DATE DUE

VACCINES

Preventing Disease

These and other books are included in the
Encyclopedia of Discovery and Invention series:

Airplanes	Movies
Anesthetics	Phonograph
Animation	Photography
Atoms	Plate Tectonics
Clocks	Printing Press
Computers	Radar
Genetics	Railroads
Germs	Ships
Gravity	Telephones
Human Origins	Telescopes
Lasers	Television
Microscopes	Vaccines

VACCINES
Preventing Disease

by MICHAEL C. BURGE
and DON NARDO

107211

The ENCYCLOPEDIA of
D·I·S·C·O·V·E·R·Y
and **INVENTION**

P.O. Box 289011 SAN DIEGO, CA 92198-9011

Library of Congress Cataloging-in-Publication Data

Burge, Michael C., 1950-
  Vaccines: preventing disease / by Michael C. Burge and
Don Nardo

    p. cm.—(The Encyclopedia of discovery and invention)
  Includes bibliographical references and index.
  Summary: Traces the history of vaccines from the first
vaccine, to the work of Louis Pasteur, to the hazards of
immunization, to vaccines today.
  ISBN 1-56006-223-1 (acid-free)
  1. Vaccines—History—Juvenile literature. [1. Vaccines—
History.] I. Nardo, Don. II. Title. III. Series.
QR189.B87 1992
615'.372'09—dc20   92-27851
                                                          CIP
                                                           AC

Contents

■■■

Foreword

The belief in progress has been one of the dominant forces in Western Civilization from the Scientific Revolution of the seventeenth century to the present. Embodied in the idea of progress is the conviction that each generation will be better off than the one that preceded it. Eventually, all peoples will benefit from and share in this better world. R.R. Palmer, in his *History of the Modern World*, calls this belief in progress "a kind of nonreligious faith that the conditions of human life" will continually improve as time goes on.

For over a thousand years prior to the seventeenth century, science had progressed little. Inquiry was largely discouraged, and experimentation, almost nonexistent. As a result, science became regressive and discovery was ignored. Benjamin Farrington, a historian of science, characterized it this way: "Science had failed to become a real force in the life of society. Instead there had arisen a conception of science as a cycle of liberal studies for a privileged minority. Science ceased to be a means of transforming the conditions of life." In short, had this intellectual climate continued, humanity's future would have been little more than a clone of its past.

Fortunately, these circumstances were not destined to last. By the seventeenth and eighteenth centuries, Western society was undergoing radical and favorable changes. And the changes that occurred gave rise to the notion that progress was a real force urging civilization forward. Surpluses of consumer goods were replacing substandard living conditions in most of Western Europe. Rigid class systems were giving way to social mobility. In nations like France and the United States, the lofty principles of democracy and popular sovereignty were being painted in broad, gilded strokes over the fading canvasses of monarchy and despotism.

But more significant than these social, economic, and political changes, the new age witnessed a rebirth of science. Centuries of scientific stagnation began crumbling before a spirit of scientific inquiry that spawned undreamed of technological advances. And it was the discoveries and inventions of scores of men and women that fueled these new technologies, dramatically increasing the ability of humankind to control nature—and, many believed, eventually to guide it.

It is a truism of science and technology that the results derived from observation and experimentation are not finalities. They are part of a process. Each discovery is but one piece in a continuum bridging past and present and heralding an extraordinary future. The heroic age of the Scientific Revolution was simply a start. It laid a foundation upon which succeeding generations of imaginative thinkers could build. It kindled the belief that progress is possible as long as there were gifted men and women who would respond to society's needs. When Antonie van Leeuwenhoek observed *Animalcules* (little animals) through his high-powered microscope in 1683, the discovery did not end there. Others followed who would call these "little animals" bacteria and, in time, recognize their role in the process of health and disease. Robert Koch, a German bacteriologist and winner of the Nobel Prize in Physiology and Medicine, was one of these men. Koch firmly established that bacteria are responsible for causing infectious diseases. He identified, among others, the causative organisms of anthrax and tuberculosis. Alexander Fleming, another Nobel Laureate, progressed still further in the quest to understand and control bacteria. In 1928, Fleming discovered penicillin, the antibiotic wonder drug. Penicillin, and the generations of antibiotics that succeeded it, have done more to prevent premature death than any other discovery in the history of humankind. And as civilization hastens toward the twenty-first century, most agree that the conquest of van Leeuwenhoek's "little animals" will continue.

The *Encyclopedia of Discovery and Invention* examines those discoveries and inventions that have had a sweeping impact on life and thought in the modern world. Each book explores the ideas that led to the invention or discovery, and, more importantly, how the world changed and continues to change because of it. The series also highlights the people behind the achievements—the unique men and women whose singular genius and rich imagination have altered the lives of everyone. Enhanced by photographs and clearly explained technical drawings, these books are comprehensive examinations of the building blocks of human progress.

VACCINES

Preventing Disease

VACCINES

Introduction

In the late 1960s the World Health Organization (WHO), an agency of the United Nations, embarked upon an ambitious and unprecedented program. The goal was the worldwide elimination of a terrifying, deadly disease called smallpox. The illness causes severe fever, chills, pain, eruptions of pus-filled sores, or pox, and very often death. For thousands of years smallpox had periodically ravaged humanity, leaving a trail of misery and death. So many people died when the disease struck ancient Rome, for example, that there were not enough wagons to carry the dead out of the city. In desperation, people threw thousands of corpses into the Tiber River.

Smallpox killed millions worldwide and remained a constant threat to humanity well into the twentieth century, despite the groundbreaking work of a British doctor named Edward Jenner. In the 1790s, Jenner discovered he could prevent smallpox by injecting people with a similar but less deadly disease. He called his discovery a vaccine. In the following century and a half scientists perfected smallpox vaccines. Many doctors in Europe, the Americas, and other parts of the world vaccinated their patients to keep them from getting the illness. And many developed, or industrialized, countries funded programs to vaccinate most of their inhabitants. In less-developed countries, ignorance, poverty, and poor medical facilities often prevented large-scale vaccination programs. So, while well-off nations like the United States had almost elimi-

... TIMELINE: **VACCINES**

1 ⟩ 2 ⟩   3 ⟩ 4 ⟩

1 ■ 1717
Britain's Lady Mary Wortley Montagu witnesses a smallpox inoculation in Turkey.

2 ■ 1721
A Boston doctor successfully inoculates residents against smallpox but the technique is outlawed in the city.

3 ■ 1796
Dr. Edward Jenner successfully vaccinates a young boy against smallpox in England using a vaccine made from cowpox.

4 ■ 1801
President Thomas Jefferson inoculates his own family with Jenner's vaccine.

5 ■ 1879
Louis Pasteur discovers the principle of attenuating germs to make a vaccine.

6 ■ 1881
Pasteur demonstrates his successful anthrax vaccine.

7 ■ 1885
Pasteur successfully vaccinates a child against rabies.

8 ■ 1892
First diphtheria vaccine goes into general use.

9 ■ 1908
Elie Metchnikoff and Paul Ehrlich receive the Nobel Prize for explaining how immunity works.

nated, or eradicated, smallpox by 1945, the disease continued to ravage other parts of the world. In that year in India, for example, the government reported at least 287,000 smallpox cases. And as late as 1967 the world experienced ten million cases of the illness, one-fifth of them fatal.

WHO officials believed that because effective smallpox vaccines were available the disease could be beaten. What had been missing in the past, they reasoned, was an international effort. The agency pledged itself to that effort and sent out teams of doctors to vaccinate people whenever and wherever outbreaks of the illness were reported. The elimination of smallpox occurred with astonishing swiftness. By October 1977 the last known case of the disease was reported in Africa, and WHO declared smallpox eradicated. This remains the only deadly disease that has been completely eliminated.

Vaccines offer hope for the eradication of other diseases. Over the years scientists have developed vaccines for many illnesses, and many of these have proven effective. But none has been as effective on a worldwide scale as the smallpox vaccine.

WHO showed that vaccines can be totally effective weapons against disease if used in a coordinated global program. Recent and exciting research into new ways of making and using vaccines also offers hope for the future. Some doctors believe that the simple discovery made by Jenner and perfected by his successors will someday make a disease-free world possible.

5 > 6 > 7 > 8 > 9 > 10 > 11 > 12 > 13 > 14 > 15 > 16 > 17 > 18 >

10 ■ 1916
The United States is struck by its first major polio epidemic.

11 ■ 1935
Two unsuccessful polio vaccines are withdrawn from use.

12 ■ 1948
Scientists declare all-out war on polio.

13 ■ 1949
John F. Enders and his colleagues discover how to grow virus cultures in the laboratory.

14 ■ 1953
Jonas Salk succeeds in making an effective polio vaccine using dead germs.

15 ■ 1961
Albert B. Sabin's polio vaccine using live germs goes into widespread use.

16 ■ 1977
The last known case of smallpox is reported from Africa.

17 ■ 1986
The first subunit vaccine, for hepatitis B, goes into general use.

18 ■ 1992
Researchers desperately attempt to find a vaccine for AIDS.

CHAPTER 1

In the Shadow of Death

The process of vaccinating patients to cure or prevent disease developed mainly in the nineteenth century. Yet the basic principle behind vaccination—using physical samples of a disease to fight a disease—was known in many ancient cultures. The ancients did not know why patients treated with such samples often recovered. Because they were unaware that microscopic organisms called germs cause disease, they did not know how and why people got sick. Nor did they understand the physical and chemical processes the human body uses to fight disease. Ancient healers usually had to resort to a process of trial and error to find cures. Sometimes they discovered cures by accident. When they found an effective cure they told others about it, and the knowledge spread to other villages and eventually to other lands. In this way early healers

Ancient healers desperately sought cures for diseases that ravaged their societies. What few successes they had usually resulted through trial and error.

provided clues about fighting disease that led modern researchers to the discovery of vaccines.

The Chinese Battle Smallpox

One of the most important clues to successfully fighting disease came from the Chinese. More than a thousand years ago Chinese doctors noticed something curious about disease. They observed that a person could contract, or catch, certain illnesses, the common cold for instance, over and over again. On the other hand, other illnesses, such as smallpox, usually struck a person only once and never returned.

For thousands of years smallpox had ravaged whole regions of China, nearly always leaving its devastating mark. A case of the disease started with a headache, pains, and fever and then covered its victim's body, throat, and mouth with burning sores. Victims suffered uncontrollable spasms and sometimes internal bleeding. The worst form of smallpox caused hemorrhaging, or severe bleeding, behind the nose and eyes, and ended with the sufferer spitting up blood. No one who reached this stage of the disease survived.

Because people could carry smallpox for several weeks before showing any symptoms, they could infect others before realizing that they themselves had the illness. Smallpox was so common for so long in China that no one knows how many people the disease killed. Historians estimate that one out of every four people who contracted it died, and many who survived suffered scars, crippling, or blindness. The Chinese observed something else about the

survivors. For some unexplained reason nearly all of those who lived through a bout with smallpox never caught it again.

Over the years Chinese healers devised a way of fighting smallpox that was sometimes effective. How the method developed remains unclear. Probably, doctors saw that survivors who suffered only mild symptoms of the illness were just as safe from later attacks as those who almost died from it. Therefore, any exposure to smallpox was enough to keep the disease from returning. The doctors must have decided that some exposure to the illness was worth the risk if it could guarantee that a person would never contract it again.

After years of careful observation and experimentation, Chinese healers developed an elaborate ceremony designed to ward off serious cases of smallpox. In this ritual children inhaled a powder into their nostrils through ivory tubes. The powder consisted of ground scabs that had formed on the bodies of smallpox victims who had suffered only mild symptoms of the disease. A few days after inhaling the powder, the children also began to develop smallpox sores and fever. In most cases their bouts with the illness were relatively mild. The important thing was that these children never had to worry again about catching the dreaded disease.

Strengthening the Body's Natural Defenses

Chinese healers did not know at the time that their methods of fighting smallpox were based on a biological process called immunity. Modern doctors define immunity as the process by

Despite limited scientific knowledge, healers in some ancient civilizations found ways to prevent some diseases.

which the body resists disease. The body can acquire immunity naturally, as in the case of a smallpox victim who survives and then is safe from further attacks of the disease. Or the body can acquire immunity artificially. This practice, in which a doctor deliberately infects a person with a form of a disease in order to ward off future attacks, is called inoculation. People who are inoculated with a disease build up a tolerance for, or ability to withstand, that disease. Inoculation can also help build up a tolerance for certain poisons.

Like the ancient Chinese, early healers in other parts of the world used these concepts without understanding how or why they actually worked. In seventh-century India, for example, Buddhist monks sometimes purposely swallowed small amounts of snake venom, a powerful poison. According to descrip-

tions in surviving ancient writings, their intention was to become immune to snakebites. When they were successful, doctors now understand, it was because they had slowly built up a tolerance to the venom.

Some ancient African healers learned to induce, or bring on, a similar tolerance for smallpox. This method, passed down through untold generations of tribal doctors, consisted of having a patient swallow smallpox scabs. A variation was to scratch the patient's skin and insert fluid from a live smallpox sore. These patients, like the Chinese children who inhaled smallpox-infected powders, almost always contracted smallpox. Many developed only mild cases of the disease and never caught it again.

Without realizing it all of these early healers had artificially stimulated the body's immune system. Using primitive forms of inoculation they had helped the body strengthen its natural defenses and develop immunity against poison or disease. Nevertheless, the use of inoculation was not systematic or widespread. And because healers who did use the process did not understand how it worked, they sometimes used the wrong dosages and ended up killing their patients. Thus, despite the fact that some people developed immunity and survived, most of those bitten by poisonous snakes died, and smallpox epidemics continued to kill thousands.

Experiment in Turkey

Periodic smallpox epidemics struck Europe in the 1300s. The epidemics struck again in the following centuries, and by the 1600s the disease killed an estimated 400,000 people a year, most of them under the age of ten. This deadly onslaught continued as new generations of victims with no tolerance for the illness were exposed to it. European doctors, who had never heard of or who rejected the work of Chinese healers, had no idea how to cure or prevent the disease.

Eventually Europeans began to discover important clues to the prevention of smallpox. In 1716 the poet Lady Mary Wortley Montagu accompanied her husband to his new post as the British ambassador to Turkey. Lady Montagu herself had been badly scarred by smallpox as a child and had lost a brother to the disease. She feared losing her own children to the fever and pain of smallpox, so she was especially intrigued by a scene she witnessed shortly after arriving in the Turkish cap-

ital of Constantinople (now Istanbul) in 1717. In the company of a Turkish acquaintance, she attended a gathering of about fifteen people in a local home. There she watched a primitive form of smallpox inoculation that the Turks referred to as engrafting. Lady Montagu was unaware that this process was very similar to ancient Chinese and African smallpox preventions and may have been copied from them.

"There is a set of old women," Lady Montagu later wrote in a letter to a

The English noblewoman Lady Mary Wortley Montagu witnessed miraculous successes with smallpox inoculation in Turkey and brought word of these practices home to Britain.

friend in Britain, "who make it their business to perform the operation every autumn, in the month of September, when the great heat is abated [lessened]." As Lady Montagu looked on in fascination, one old woman opened a vein in a person's arm. After dipping a needle into a nutshell filled with pus from smallpox sores, the old woman inserted the instrument into the open vein. She then repeated the procedure, injecting disease samples into several more veins.

Describing the results of the procedure, Lady Montagu wrote that the patients seemed perfectly healthy for a few days. "Then the fever begins to seize them, and they keep to their beds two days, very seldom three." Lady Montagu was amazed that the seemingly dangerous treatment, performed annually on thousands of Turks, was successful in most cases. A majority of patients gained permanent immunity to smallpox without serious suffering. "There is no example of anyone that has died in it," she wrote, "and you may believe I am very well satisfied of the safety of this experiment, since I intend to try it on my dear little son."

True to her word, while still living in Constantinople, Lady Montagu had her son inoculated, and he survived with no ill effects. Four years later, after the Montagus had returned to London, a smallpox epidemic broke out, and Lady Montagu realized that her daughter was at risk. In 1721, under the observation of three doctors and several newspaper reporters, Lady Montagu's daughter was inoculated. Medical authorities closely watched and reported the progress of the young girl's disease. When she survived, inoculation as a means of controlling smallpox captured the city's attention. London was abuzz with this new notion of infecting people, particularly children, with an apparently mild case of smallpox to prevent them from catching a fatal or disabling case later.

A Princess Takes Interest in Inoculation

One Londoner who took a great deal of interest in this practice was Princess Caroline, the wife of the future king George II. The princess wanted to protect her children through the new technique, but she insisted on being absolutely sure it was safe. As an experiment she offered a chance for freedom to six convicts who had been sentenced to die by hanging. All they had to do was submit to smallpox inoculation, and the survivors would go free. After agreeing to the deal the six men received their inoculations. Five of them contracted the disease and survived in good shape, while the sixth never caught it, probably because he had previously had the disease. As she had promised, the princess ordered that all six men be set free.

Princess Caroline was still uncertain that the technique was safe enough to use on her own children. She ordered a group of London orphans to be inoculated. When all of them survived as well, she was satisfied that the process was indeed safe. She had her two daughters inoculated, and they survived with no ill effects. Now that the future queen of the British Empire endorsed the new practice, the rest of the British were also convinced. Inoculation with smallpox samples spread throughout Great Britain and across the English Channel to the European continent.

The Boston Epidemic

Eventually smallpox inoculation also caught on in the Americas. Millions of native American people had died from smallpox during the 1500s, 1600s, and 1700s after being infected by European colonists who unwittingly carried the disease. But the new settlers had managed to avoid any major epidemics in their own communities, probably as a result of their small numbers. Because they wanted to keep it that way, small cities like Boston tried to isolate anyone known to be carrying smallpox. Inevitably, however, smallpox gained a foothold. In May 1721—the same year Lady Montagu introduced inoculation to London—a smallpox epidemic hit Boston. While many residents panicked and fled the city, one influential man, the Reverend Cotton Mather, suggested trying inoculation.

Mather had first learned about inoculation in 1706, when he quizzed one of his African slaves about diseases the slave had had before arriving in the colonies. When Mather asked about smallpox the slave told him he had

Princess Caroline (left), the wife of Britain's future king George II (right), saw great promise in smallpox inoculation. But before using the technique on her own children, she tested it on a group of convicts and orphans.

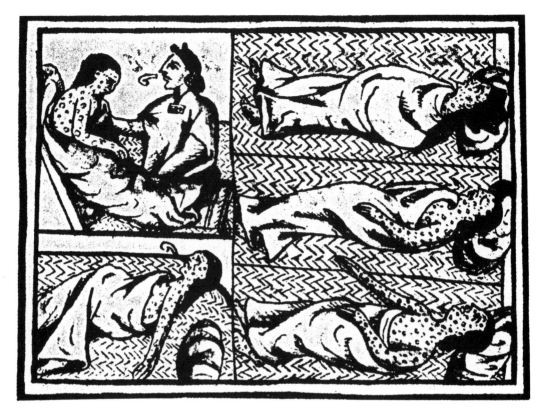

A historical illustration depicts the suffering endured by native Americans who contracted smallpox from European explorers. Although smallpox devastated the societies of many native peoples, some discovered and practiced inoculation. Rev. Cotton Mather learned of this from an African man who was his slave.

been inoculated by his tribe in Africa. The man showed Mather his arm, which bore a small circular inoculation scar. Mather recalled this incident years later when he came across an article written by Dr. Emanuel Timonius. Timonius, who had been present at the inoculation of Lady Montagu's son in Constantinople, highly recommended using inoculation to fight smallpox.

During the 1721 Boston outbreak of smallpox, Mather tried to interest local doctors in the idea of inoculation. Most of them were unfamiliar with the process and skeptical about its supposed benefits. Mather then approached his friend, Dr. Zabdiel Boylston, about his

slave's story and Timonius's article.

Boylston took immediate interest in the idea of inoculation. In July 1721 he took scabs from some of his smallpox patients and ground them into a fine powder. He tested the substance on an adult slave, the slave's two-and-a-half-year-old son, and his own six-year-old son as well.

Boylston's experiment was a success. Those he had inoculated survived and appeared to be immune to smallpox. Mather was greatly impressed and spoke out publicly in favor of inoculation. But community leaders were angry that Boylston had risked spreading the disease and frightened that inoculation

As the title page of Dr. Zabdiel Boylston's book about smallpox inoculation explains, the book contains "directions to the unexperienced."

oculating patients, had found that although most developed mild cases of smallpox and survived, a few patients developed violent cases and died. Boylston could not explain why some people died or predict who was most at risk.

Despite the risk Mather decided to have Samuel inoculated, and the young man survived. This success did not stem the unreasonable and growing fear among Bostonians that Mather and Boylston were somehow making the epidemic worse. When word of Samuel's inoculation reached the community, that fear exploded into violence. Someone threw a bomb through Mather's window in the middle of the night. No one was injured, and despite the incident, Mather strongly continued to advocate inoculation.

Mather often spoke publicly and forcefully about the benefits of smallpox inoculation.

might somehow backfire and kill those who had received it. They outlawed the technique on July 22, 1721.

Soon afterward Mather's son Samuel returned home from Harvard College with news that his roommate had contracted smallpox and died. Samuel begged his father to have him inoculated, which put Mather in a desperate spot. First, the practice was illegal. Also, there was a chance that if Samuel was inoculated, he might die. Boylston, who had continued quietly in-

A BRIEF RULE

To guide the Common People of

NEW-ENGLAND

How to order themselves and theirs in the

Small Pocks, or Measels.

A concerned writer outlines the symptoms of smallpox and measles and urges New England residents to take proper precautions against both when symptoms appear.

After the well-publicized smallpox inoculations in Britain and Boston in the 1720s, the technique became common in Europe and in the American colonies. But inoculation was by no means foolproof in checking the spread of the disease. In fact people who had never been inoculated often contracted smallpox after coming into contact with people who had been inoculated. Because they did not know that smallpox is spread by germs, doctors did not realize that inoculated people could still spread the illness to others, even before coming down with obvious symptoms. The doctors did not recognize that inoculated people needed to be quarantined, or kept isolated from others, until fully recovered.

Debates over the merits and risks of inoculation continued through the latter half of the eighteenth century, and those who feared the technique often won these arguments. As a result, by 1790 many towns in the New England colonies and in Europe had banned the practice of inoculation. No one foresaw that an alternative to inoculation—one that offered immunity with little or no risk of disease—was possible. No one, that is, until a country doctor in England conducted an experiment with a cow and forever changed the face of medical science.

CHAPTER 2

The First Vaccine

Dr. Edward Jenner's discovery of the first vaccine stands as one of the most significant breakthroughs in the history of medicine. A vaccine is a substance made from disease germs. A person who is inoculated with a vaccine derived from a certain disease gains temporary or permanent immunity to that disease. Jenner developed a vaccine for smallpox. What makes his achievement especially remarkable is that he worked without the sophisticated tools of modern scientists. Jenner made his discovery using little more than natural cu-

A healthy curiosity, keen powers of observation, a logical mind, and the painful memory of his own bout with smallpox led Dr. Edward Jenner to discover the first vaccine.

riosity and his powers of observation and logic.

Jenner derived his smallpox vaccine in 1796 from cowpox, a disease similar in many ways to smallpox. An important difference is that cowpox sickens or kills cows but is relatively harmless to humans. Human cases of cowpox, which occurred sometimes among farmers and dairy workers in Jenner's time, usually produce nothing more than a rash, mild fever, headache, and muscle aches. These are some of the same symptoms that occur in a very mild case of smallpox. Through a simple experiment Jenner proved that a human who contracts cowpox becomes immune to smallpox nearly for life. Jenner's cowpox vaccine also eliminated the risk of catching smallpox from smallpox inoculations.

Starved and Bled in a Barn

Jenner became interested in studying smallpox because of his frightening boyhood experience with the disease. He was born in 1749 in Berkeley, England, in County Gloucestershire, not far from the Welsh border. Jenner became an orphan at the age of five. His older brother Stephen took him in and raised him as one of his own children. In 1757, when Edward Jenner was eight, a smallpox epidemic raged through the British Isles, and Stephen sent the boy to the nearby village of Wotton-on-Edge to be inoculated. The inoculation process Jenner experienced was nothing like the one Lady Montagu had witnessed in Turkey forty years earlier.

Before the inoculation took place Jenner had to undergo a period of starvation. He also had to endure the process of bleeding, in which someone opened one of his veins and allowed some of his blood to flow out into a bowl. This once-common practice was based on the false belief that blood contains "impurities." Supposedly, removing blood also removed many of these so-called impurities and made a person healthier. Jenner later recalled, "There was bleeding till the blood was thin; purging [losing weight] till the body was wasted to a skeleton; and starving on [a] vegetable diet to keep it so." At the time

Sophisticated microscopes provide a unique view of smallpox germs (pictured). Jenner did not have the benefit of such microscopes, making his discovery all the more fantastic.

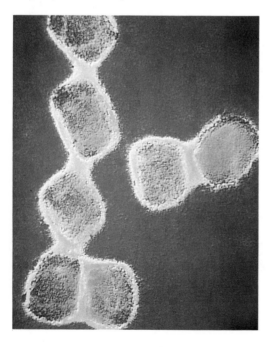

the doctors and druggists who practiced inoculation believed that starving and bleeding strengthened the body, enabling it to better withstand disease.

After being starved and bled Jenner was taken to a barn with a group of boys roughly his own age. In the barn were several other boys who had been inoculated a week or two earlier. Some of them had broken out in smallpox sores and suffered from fever and other symptoms of the disease. Soon after the boys in Jenner's group arrived, a druggist scratched wounds into their arms with a knife and affixed smallpox scabs to the cuts. The boys waited, in hunger and discomfort, for the week or two required for the disease to take hold. Soon they developed open sores, nausea, and fever—all symptoms of smallpox. Weeks later, after the sores dried to scabs and fell from their skin, the boys were allowed to leave the barn. Young Jenner took with him two things: lifelong immunity to smallpox and the undying memory of the worst experience of his life.

Mystery of the Milkmaids

Edward Jenner later became a doctor. Remembering his own terrible experience with smallpox, he hoped someday to help find a cure for the illness. Jenner carefully observed the cases of smallpox that he encountered, accumulating whatever information he could about the disease. During his early years of practice in Gloucestershire, he heard some local farmers make an unusual claim. According to the farmers, young girls and others who regularly milked cows, and who came down with cowpox, later displayed immunity to smallpox.

This made Jenner recall hearing the same rumor years before while in the company of the doctor to whom he had been apprenticed. While bandaging a young milkmaid's finger the doctor had lectured her about the dangers of catching smallpox. "Never know who'll be next," warned the doctor. "Could be anybody. Could be you! Then that pretty skin of yours wouldn't look so pretty." The girl then insisted that she could not catch smallpox. When asked why she replied, "I've had the cowpox!" The doctor, who thought this was an ignorant superstition, only laughed. "Ed-

Farmers in England's Gloucestershire region claimed that young girls and others who regularly milked cows frequently and mysteriously displayed an immunity to smallpox after coming down with cowpox.

ward, you hear that?" he asked Jenner. "Don't forget it! Whenever you go visiting your patients, take a cow with you! Wonderful animal, the cow!"

When the adult Jenner heard the story of the milkmaids repeated a number of times, he asked some other local doctors about it. Like his mentor, Jenner's colleagues assumed it was superstition and dismissed it. But Jenner was not so sure. In time, he heard the story so often that he thought it might have some basis in fact.

The Farmer and the Cow

For several years Jenner took careful notes on cowpox cases and studied how the disease passed from cows to humans. In 1778 he heard that a farmer named William Smith had contracted cowpox after milking his cow. Jenner went to Smith's farm to investigate and discovered that the cow's udders had been covered with cowpox sores while Smith was milking it. Apparently the farmer had caught the disease when pus from the sores entered open cuts on his hands. Jenner knew that smallpox also entered people's bodies through cuts in the skin during inoculations.

Jenner now tried to piece together a theory from the information he had gathered. He knew that the symptoms of cowpox and mild smallpox were very similar and that they could be contracted in the same way. It seemed logical to Jenner, therefore, that smallpox and cowpox were different forms of the same disease. This, he concluded, would not only explain their similarities, but also account for the stories of people gaining immunity to smallpox

after bouts of cowpox. Contracting the milder form of the disease—cowpox—might have the same immunizing effect as a mild case of smallpox induced by inoculation.

Jenner's theory that smallpox and cowpox were versions of the same disease was incorrect. Yet his wrong guess set him on the right track. Believing that catching cowpox did indeed provide immunity to smallpox, he took the next logical step. If contracting cowpox naturally created immunity, he reasoned, artificially contracting the disease should do the same. Therefore, it should be possible to inoculate people with cowpox to make them immune to smallpox. Jenner wrote in 1793:

> During the investigation of the casual [naturally acquired] cowpox, I was struck by the idea that it might be practicable to propagate [breed] the disease by inoculation, after the manner of the smallpox, first from the cow, and finally from one human being to another.

A Dangerous Experiment

Jenner first tested his theory in 1796. He needed two subjects, one infected with cowpox, the other healthy. Jenner intended to take infected pus from the ill subject and use it to infect the healthy subject with cowpox. A young milkmaid named Sarah Nelmes, who had recently contracted cowpox, and an eight-year-old boy named James Phipps agreed to take part in the experiment. Wrote Jenner:

> The more accurately to observe the progress of the infection I selected a healthy boy, about eight years old, for the purpose of inoculating for cowpox. The [cowpox] matter was taken from a

sore on the hand of a dairymaid, who was infected by her master's cows, and it was inserted on the 14th day of May, 1796, into the arm of the boy by means of two superficial incisions [shallow cuts] . . . each about an inch long.

Seven days after receiving the inoculation Phipps came down with cowpox. After a single day of minor symptoms, including slight chills and headache, the sickness passed and the boy was once more his healthy self. Jenner was now ready for the next and most important part of the test. In order to see if Phipps's cowpox inoculation had given

Jenner's illustration of the cowpox-infected hand of milkmaid Sarah Nelmes. Jenner injected fluid from these sores into a healthy boy in hopes of giving the boy immunity against smallpox.

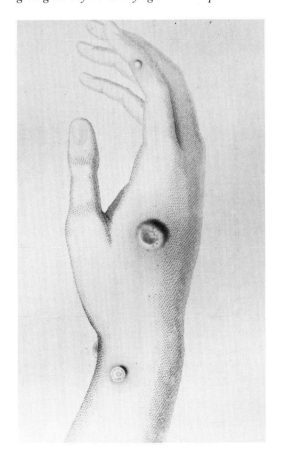

him immunity to smallpox, Jenner had to infect the boy with smallpox. This was potentially dangerous, because if Jenner's theory was wrong, the boy might contract a serious case of smallpox and die. Despite the risks the experiment proceeded. As Jenner later described it:

> In order to ascertain whether the boy, after feeling so slight an affection of the system [sickness] from the cowpox virus, was secure from the contagion of the smallpox, he was inoculated the 1st of July . . . with variolous matter [smallpox pus], immediately taken from a pustule [open sore]. Several slight punctures and incisions were made on both his arms, and the matter was carefully inserted.

Jenner waited nervously to see if the boy would contract smallpox. When Phipps remained healthy for several weeks, the doctor was sure that the danger had passed. Jenner happily wrote to a friend, explaining how he had inoculated the boy with cowpox, and added:

> But now listen to the most delightful part of my story. The boy has since been inoculated for the smallpox, which, as I ventured to predict, produced no effects. I shall now pursue my experiments with redoubled ardour [passion].

The dangerous experiment had succeeded. Jenner had proven that inoculation with the relatively harmless cowpox could protect a person from catching the dreaded smallpox. This provided an effective alternative to regular smallpox inoculation, with its risk of serious infection and death. Jenner foresaw that, if enough people worldwide received this new kind of inoculation, smallpox might eventually be elimi-

Jenner vaccinates eight-year-old James Phipps against smallpox. After receiving an injection of cowpox, Phipps became ill with the disease. Jenner then injected the boy with smallpox but Phipps remained healthy. The vaccine had succeeded.

nated. He wrote about the "joy I felt at the prospect before me of being the instrument destined to take away from the world one of its greatest calamities."

Doubt and Condemnation

Jenner realized that the first step toward widespread use of his treatment was to inform the medical community and public of the results of his experiment. In 1798, he published a sixty-four-page pamphlet entitled *From an Inquiry into the Causes and Effects of* Variolae Vaccinae, *a Disease Discovered in Some of the Western Counties of England, Particularly Gloucestershire and Known by the Name of the Cowpox.* Jenner called his new discovery a vaccine, after the Latin name for cowpox—*Variolae vaccinae.* The word *vaccine* eventually became the universal

Jenner's vaccine prompted condemnation as well as praise. An early nineteenth-century caricature depicts the earnest doctor at work surrounded by people who have undergone vaccination and been transformed into cow-like creatures.

AN

INQUIRY

INTO

THE CAUSES AND EFFECTS

OF

THE VARIOLÆ VACCINÆ,

A DISEASE

DISCOVERED IN SOME OF THE WESTERN COUNTIES OF ENGLAND,

PARTICULARLY

GLOUCESTERSHIRE,

AND KNOWN BY THE NAME OF

THE COW POX.

BY EDWARD JENNER, M. D. F. R. S. &c.

—— QUID NOBIS CERTIUS IPSIS
SENSIBUS ESSE POTEST, QUO VERA AC FALSA NOTEMUS.

LUCRETIUS.

London:

PRINTED, FOR THE AUTHOR,

BY SAMPSON LOW, N°. 7, BERWICK STREET, SOHO:

AND SOLD BY LAW, AVE-MARIA LANE; AND MURRAY AND HIGHLEY, FLEET STREET

1798.

The title page from Jenner's pamphlet on vaccination. In it he established the thesis that vaccination with cowpox provides immunity against smallpox.

term for any agent that provides protection against a specific disease by triggering the body's immune system without passing on the disease itself.

Jenner's pamphlet quickly became famous in Great Britain and in other parts of Europe. While some people thought his discovery sounded hopeful, many others immediately voiced opposition to the idea of vaccination. Some who adhered to the age-old belief that diseases were punishments sent by God condemned Jenner for trying to interfere in God's work. One of Jenner's critics explained:

> Smallpox is a visitation from God and originates [grows] in man, but the cowpox is produced by presumptuous, impious men. The former [smallpox] Heaven ordained, the latter [cowpox] is perhaps a daring and profane violation of our holy order.

Doctors also debated the merits of the new technique. Some scolded Jenner for wasting his time trying to prove that a superstition was true. Other doctors were skeptical of Jenner's results because he had successfully performed his experiment only once. This might have been a lucky accident, they said, and the test would have to be repeated many times to confirm that the treatment was sound.

Confirmation was not long in coming. A British cattle breeder named Benjamin Jesty publicly revealed that he had performed a similar experiment in 1774. He too had heard the story of the milkmaids who seemed immune to smallpox. So he had exposed all of the members of his family to cowpox in an attempt to prevent their catching smallpox. He had been successful, but for reasons of his own he had told no one about his experiment. Although Jesty's work preceded Jenner's, Jenner received credit for the discovery of the smallpox vaccination because he was the first to publish his findings. Other confirmations of the treatment's effectiveness followed the publication of Jenner's pamphlet. Doctors in Great Britain and other parts of Europe repeated Jenner's test and obtained similar favorable results. Vaccination rapidly

A woman holds her child steady as Jenner vaccinates the child. Despite Jenner's successes, vaccination faced many obstacles before being accepted as a safe and routine medical practice.

replaced inoculation as the preferred way to prevent smallpox in many parts of Europe and soon afterward in the Americas.

Jenner's Remarkable Legacy

Jenner left behind an important and remarkable legacy. Without intending to he laid the foundation for an entirely new branch of science—immunology—devoted to the study of the body's immune system. At the time, Jenner and other doctors knew almost nothing about how the immune system worked. They did not know that germs caused cowpox, smallpox, and other diseases and did not understand why vaccination provided immunity. Future immunologists and biologists would build on the experiments of Jenner and his colleagues. They would learn the causes of many diseases and find new ways to use the body's immune system to fight those diseases.

It would be a slow, painstaking process. The battle against smallpox, for instance, had only just begun. Jenner had provided an important weapon in the fight, but it would take nearly two hundred years for his dream of eradicating the disease to become a reality. In the

Despite his groundbreaking findings, Jenner fought an uphill battle to convince some people of the merits of vaccines.

meantime Jenner faced another difficult, and very personal, battle. Although vaccination had caught on quickly with many doctors, a number of influential scientists and politicians still opposed the technique. Jenner would spend a great deal of time and energy defending the concept of vaccination in what would become the fight of his life.

A Battle for Acceptance

Edward Jenner's vaccine offered new hope against the killer disease smallpox. In the years following the publication of his pamphlet describing his experiment, many doctors in Europe and other areas began vaccinating their patients. A number of doctors and scientists felt that vaccination might someday prove effective against other diseases too.

Not everyone was so optimistic about the new technique of vaccination. One group of influential people, especially, saw the technique as a threat to the established natural order of the late-eighteenth- and early-nineteenth-century world. Most of the members of this group were highly educated British clergymen, writers, scientists, and politicians. Their chief spokesman was the well-known clergyman-turned-economist—Thomas Malthus.

Fear of Overpopulation

Malthus's and his colleagues' objections to vaccination stemmed mainly from their alarm over certain large-scale social changes taking place in Great Britain. At the time, the country was undergoing the effects of the Industrial Revolution, which had begun in the mid-1700s. Be-

Nurses care for smallpox patients in an English smallpox hospital. Doctors around the world saw promise in vaccines. But for those who had already contracted the disease, vaccines offered no hope.

During the Industrial Revolution many rural residents moved to the cities in search of factory jobs. The huge influx of people put great burdens on the cities.

fore this revolution the economies of nations were based primarily on rural agriculture. But the invention of new, complex machines and other mechanical devices had caused Great Britain and some other countries to shift their centers of production to factories in cities. As a result of this shift many people from the countryside migrated to the cities in search of jobs. The cities of that time were not prepared for this sudden and huge influx of people, most of whom were poor. Huge slums grew up around London and other cities. Often, the crowded, filthy tenement houses had no running water and no garbage or sewage facilities. These unhealthy conditions promoted the spread of deadly contagious diseases like typhus, cholera, and smallpox.

Malthus believed that these new surges in population were dangerous to the British economy and to established society. Most of the poor urban workers contributed little or nothing to society, Malthus argued, and struggled to make simply enough money to eat and survive. He feared that these people would continue reproducing and growing in number until farmers could no longer grow enough food to sustain everyone in society. In other words, the world's growing population would eventually outgrow its food supply. Then, suggested Malthus, there would be mass starvation and chaos, and society would collapse into a primitive state.

Therefore, said Malthus, society needed certain controls, which he called checks, to keep the population from rising too high. The most efficient checks, Malthus and his colleagues believed, were naturally recurring ones such as war, famine, and disease. According to this view society needed occasional plagues and epidemics to help check adverse population growth. Diseases like smallpox were, in the long run, beneficial rather than damaging to society.

Encouraging the Spread of Disease

Malthus published his ideas about population in 1798, the same year Jenner's pamphlet appeared, in a book called *An Essay on the Principle of Population*. In the book Malthus argued against protecting the poor from smallpox and other deadly diseases. Society should do just the opposite, he said, since limiting the number of poor, unproductive people is in society's best interest. Wrote Malthus:

> Instead of recommending cleanliness to the poor we should encourage contrary habits. In our towns we should make the streets narrower, crowd more people into the houses, and court the return of the [bubonic] plague. In the country, we should build our villages near stagnant [unmoving] pools [where diseases easily breed], and particularly encourage settlements in all marshy and unwholesome situations. But above all, [we should] reprobate [condemn] specific remedies for ravaging diseases, and those benevolent, but much mistaken men, who have thought they were doing a service to mankind by projecting schemes for the total extirpation [elimination] of particular disorders.

Malthus and others who had this attitude toward disease were naturally disturbed about Jenner's discovery of an effective smallpox vaccine. As Jenner's technique began to catch on with many doctors, Malthus and others spoke out vigorously against the idea of vaccination. In a revised 1806 version of his

Thomas Malthus spoke forcefully against vaccines. He viewed disease as a natural means of population control.

book, Malthus attacked Jenner's vaccine, saying:

> Nature will not, nor cannot be defeated in her purposes. The necessary mortality must come, in some form or another; and the extirpation of one disease will only be the signal for the birth of another perhaps more fatal. . . . If we stop up any of these channels, it is most perfectly clear that the stream of mortality must run with greater force through some of the other channels. . . . The smallpox is certainly one of these channels, and a very broad one, which Nature has opened for the last thousand years, to keep the population down to the level of the means of subsistence; but had this been closed, others would have become wider or new ones had been formed.

According to Malthus, eradicating smallpox was a waste of time, because nature would only provide a new killer disease to take its place.

Dr. Johann Peter Frank vaccinated a group of Austrian children and then persuaded the government to support vaccination for everyone.

Recognition and Financial Support

Jenner, like most doctors of his day, strongly disagreed with Malthus's views. Jenner argued that it was society's duty to eliminate dread diseases and ease the suffering of all people, including the poor. Defending vaccination, Jenner urged, "Yes, be vaccinated. Instead of waiting for the disease to attack us and then to worry about its cause and cure, let us prevent the disease from ever striking us." Jenner thought that Malthus's fears of an overpopulation catastrophe were exaggerated. What disturbed Jenner more was that Malthus and others seemed so willing to see people suffer from smallpox. "I hope," remarked Jenner, "that some day the practice of producing cowpox in human beings will spread over the whole world. When that day comes there will be no more smallpox."

While Malthus and his colleagues opposed Jenner and his work, other influential people supported the idea of vaccination and heartily praised Jenner. In 1800 in Vienna, Austria, for example, Dr. Johann Peter Frank, director of the city's general hospital, heard about doctors vaccinating themselves during an epidemic. Soon afterward Frank vaccinated a number of Viennese children with the new vaccine. He then persuaded the Austrian government to support vaccination for the rest of the city's population.

Napoleon Bonaparte, ruler of France, was so impressed by Jenner's discovery that he bestowed on the doctor France's highest award. Napoleon's

Napoleon Bonaparte, France's powerful emperor, expressed great admiration for Edward Jenner and his discovery.

French citizens flock to the Paris Academy of Medicine to receive their vaccinations.

admiration for Jenner never waned. A few years later, when France and Britain were at war, Napoleon received a British petition asking for the release of prisoners. "No, no!" insisted Napoleon. "Release those English prisoners? Never!" Then someone told him that Edward Jenner had signed the petition. "Ah, we can refuse nothing to that name," said France's ruler, and he released the prisoners.

Jenner received a great deal of support in Great Britain, too. The British army and navy both ordered that all soldiers and sailors be vaccinated. The prestigious Oxford University gave Jenner an honorary doctor of medicine degree, and the country's ruling body,

Parliament, granted him large sums of money to continue his research.

Despite Parliament's recognition and financial support of Jenner, British leaders were not prepared to authorize widespread vaccination of the population. This was because Malthus's arguments about the need to check the growth of the poor masses continued to sway influential members of Parliament. Year after year the ruling body refused to approve funds for nationwide vaccination. Even many years later, in 1853, when Parliament finally passed laws requiring that all British be vaccinated, it still refused to approve the money necessary to implement those laws effectively.

The Vaccine in the Americas

While debate about vaccination continued in Europe, word of Jenner's work spread throughout the Americas. In the United States Harvard University professor Dr. Benjamin Waterhouse quickly grasped the potential of the new vaccine to prevent smallpox. Waterhouse contacted Jenner, telling him of his desire to try vaccination. But, the American doctor explained, cows in the Americas did not carry cowpox, probably because, living on another continent, they had never been exposed to the disease. Therefore, Waterhouse had no cowpox samples to work with. Jenner gladly sent Waterhouse a string soaked in cowpox, which could be used to infect cows and create a supply of cowpox pus. In 1800 Waterhouse began

Dr. Benjamin Waterhouse contacted Jenner to say that he wanted to bring the smallpox vaccine to America.

President John Adams expressed interest in vaccines but did little to promote their use.

his vaccination campaign by successfully treating members of his own family. Waterhouse quickly spread the news of vaccination. He wrote the pamphlet *A Prospect of Extinguishing the Small-Pox* and sent a copy to U.S. president John Adams. Adams expressed interest in the concept but offered little real support.

However, Thomas Jefferson, who succeeded Adams as president in 1801, played an active role in promoting vaccination. He asked Waterhouse for a supply of cowpox fluid and instructions on how to administer the vaccine. Jefferson then vaccinated many of his relatives and friends. In November 1801 Jefferson wrote:

> I inoculated about seventy or eighty of my family; my sons-in-law about as many of theirs, and including our neighbors who wished to avail themselves of the opportunity, our whole experiment extended to about two hundred persons.

Also in 1801, Jefferson wrote a congratulatory letter to Jenner, saying, "You have erased from the calendar of hu-

Thomas Jefferson, who succeeded Adams as president, strongly supported vaccination and hastened its acceptance.

man afflictions one of its greatest. Yours is the comfortable reflection that mankind can never forget that you have lived." Jefferson's support helped popularize the treatment, and word of vaccination spread rapidly throughout the Americas. Doctors in many North and South American cities flooded Jenner and other European colleagues with requests for samples of the vaccine.

The Difficulties of Shipping the Vaccine

Problems in transporting the samples soon arose. Although sending a soaked thread worked sometimes, it was not a reliable method. The vaccine did not retain its potency for long outside of the warm, moist environment of a living body. At the time, travel between continents took many days or weeks. Doctors found that shipping the samples in goose quills or glass bottles worked a bit better, but these samples, too, often lost their potency for the same reason. Doctors searched for a more reliable method of shipment.

The Spanish devised one unusually elaborate yet effective method in 1802. In that year a smallpox epidemic struck the Spanish colonists in Bogotá, Colombia, in South America. Spanish authorities called upon José Felipe de Flores, a doctor who had successfully inoculated Indians in Guatemala in Central America. The authorities asked Flores to find an effective way of shipping vaccine to Colombia and other Spanish colonies.

A Human Chain

Realizing that the main problem was keeping the vaccine potent outside of living bodies, Flores suggested the novel idea of actually using human bodies as shipping containers. He proposed keeping the cowpox samples alive by vaccinating a human chain of orphans during the long ocean voyage from Europe to South America.

The first step in Flores's plan was to vaccinate one or two orphans and separate them from the others. All of the children would then board a ship bound for a faraway port. When the vaccinated children broke out in cowpox sores, someone could collect fresh fluid from the sores and use it to vaccinate another pair of orphans. By continuing this process potent samples of the vaccine might survive the long trip across the ocean. Because human cases of cowpox are so mild, said Flores, the lives of the orphans would not be at risk. This method proved extremely successful. By 1805 hundreds of thousands of Spanish colonists around the world had received the cowpox vaccine and gained immunity to smallpox.

Vaccination in War and Peace

In time, as vaccination won increasing support in many parts of the world, some countries instituted nationwide vaccination programs. The German nation of Prussia, for instance, began by vaccinating all of its soldiers in 1870 and 1871 while it was at war with France. At the time Europe was undergoing a widespread smallpox epidemic. As the disease spread through the ranks of the armies, it became clear that the army with the best vaccination program

French youth await vaccination during the Franco-Prussian War. The Prussians had a decided advantage over the French because the Prussian vaccination effort was more thorough.

would have a decided advantage. France also used vaccination on its soldiers, but its program was not as widespread or efficient as that of Prussia. The results of Prussia's better program proved dramatic. During the first six months of the war, more than 280,000 French soldiers caught smallpox and 23,470 of them died. By comparison, 8,360 Prussian soldiers caught the disease and only 297 of them died.

Prussia's program was so successful that, after the war ended, Prussian officials expanded it to the civilian population. The government undertook the task of vaccinating every child in the country at the age of two and then revaccinating them at age twelve as an extra precaution. By 1899 Prussia had slashed its rate of death from smallpox from eight thousand for every two million people to just one in two million.

The Price of Recognition

Thanks to Jenner's discovery millions of people received vaccinations and escaped the horrors of smallpox. Summing up the importance of Jenner's work, the famous Scottish physician Dr. James Simpson wrote in 1847:

> During the long European wars connected with and following the French Revolution, it has been calculated that five or six millions of human lives were lost. In Europe, vaccination has already preserved from death a greater number of human beings than were sacrificed during the course of these wars. The lancet [surgical knife] of Jenner has saved far more human lives than the sword of Napoleon destroyed.

It is a sad fact, Simpson pointed out, that governments do not always recog-

nize the importance of such life-saving work. Instead they often heap financial and other rewards on those that destroy life. Despite his great contribution, said Simpson, the British government did not give Jenner the ultimate in recognition—the funding for nationwide vaccinations. Explained Simpson:

> On these devastating European wars England lavished millions of money, and freely bestowed honors . . . and heavy annual pensions upon the soldiers who were most successful in fighting her battles and destroying their fellow-men. She grudgingly awarded Jenner with 30,000 pounds for saving 30,000 of her subjects annually [amounting to only one pound per life saved].

Dr. James Simpson (above) was dismayed by the British government's slow recognition of Jenner's life-saving work. When vaccination finally caught on, everyone wanted a turn (below).

Although only some countries instituted nationwide vaccination programs, Jenner's vaccine against smallpox re-

An engraving that appeared in Harper's Weekly *in 1870 depicts a scene that, by this time, was becoming quite common in some parts of the world.*

mained an example of how doctors might effectively fight a dangerous disease through prevention. Many other diseases besides smallpox threatened humanity. People wondered whether vaccination might eventually work with these illnesses, too. Unfortunately, initial research into other vaccines proved largely fruitless. Most other diseases were very different than smallpox, and they also spread from person to person in different ways. For a long time doctors could not conceive of ways to apply Jenner's concept of vaccination to these other diseases. The one person who eventually did find a way was not a doctor, but a French chemist, whose initial interest was not humans, but wine.

Louis Pasteur and Attenuated Vaccines

In 1854 a group of French wine makers asked their countryman, thirty-two-year-old chemist Louis Pasteur, to find out what caused wine to spoil. After conducting a number of experiments Pasteur determined that microscopic organisms, or germs, caused the spoilage. To be exact, specific kinds of germs—bacteria—were the culprits. Scientists had known about bacteria and other types of germs for centuries but had assumed that these tiny agents had no purpose in nature. Believing germs to be completely harmless, most scientists did not connect them with disease or other natural processes. But Pasteur's discovery that bacteria caused spoilage showed that this belief was wrong. He began to suspect that these mysterious organisms might be capable of much more than just spoilage. If they could damage wine, he wondered, could they also harm plants, animals, and people? As it turned out, Pasteur was right. In

Through painstaking research, French chemist Louis Pasteur confirmed that germs cause disease. During the course of this work, Pasteur also made discoveries that would advance the use and understanding of vaccines.

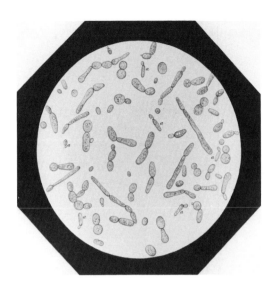

Pasteur's understanding of germs and disease grew out of his search for the cause of wine spoilage. He identified germs, specifically bacteria, as the cause of the spoiled wine.

the following years he and other scientists confirmed the germ theory, the idea that germs cause disease.

During his years of experiments involving germs and disease, Pasteur also became interested in finding ways of fighting and preventing deadly diseases. According to his biographer Madeleine Grant, in *Louis Pasteur: Fighting Hero of Science*:

> The success of Jenner's smallpox vaccine was constantly on his mind. He read about it, reasoned with it, and tried to understand it. . . . Jenner's vaccine worked, but no one could explain how. Pasteur tried to. Were the smallpox microbe [germ] and the cowpox microbe one and the same organism, or were they different? What happened to the smallpox germ when it multiplied in the cow? Did growth in the cow weaken it?

Pasteur eventually found that germs do, in fact, grow weaker under certain circumstances. The most significant as-

pect of his vaccine research was the discovery of the principle of attenuation. Pasteur showed that germs can be attenuated, or weakened, so that they do not infect their hosts but still trigger the body's immune system.

On the Trail of the Chicken Killer

Some people in Pasteur's time suggested that his landmark discovery of attenuation came mainly by chance. But Pasteur himself expressed the opinion that this was not entirely accurate. Without his extensive training and familiarity with his subject, he pointed out, he might easily have skipped over certain facts and missed drawing the right conclusion. "In the field of experimentation," he said, "chance favors only the prepared mind."

The first bit of chance occurred in 1878 when, at the request of a colleague, Pasteur temporarily put aside his regular research to consider a new problem. For a number of years, Pasteur had been studying anthrax, a disease of cattle, sheep, and other livestock. It was through isolating and describing the behavior of anthrax germs that he and other scientists had recently established the connection between germs and disease.

Pasteur was searching for a way to produce a vaccine for anthrax when the unexpected request interrupted him. Dr. H. Toussaint, a veterinary scientist, sent him the head of a rooster that had died of a disease known as chicken cholera. Toussaint believed that he had found the germ that caused the disease. To prove it and search for a cure, he needed large numbers of the germs for study and experimentation. He tried to grow a culture, a colony of several million of the germs, but was unsuccessful. He turned to Pasteur for help.

Pasteur accepted the challenge and decided to help Toussaint find a way to prevent the disease. Describing the illness, which periodically killed up to 90 percent of some French farmers' chicken flocks, Pasteur wrote:

> There sometimes appears in poultry yards a destructive disease by the name of chicken cholera. The bird affected by it is feeble, and staggers about with drooping wings. Its ruffled feathers give it the shape of a ball. It is seized with overpowering drowsiness, and if one forces it to open its eyes it appears to wake from a deep sleep; the lids soon close again, and usually death occurs after a short mute agony, without the creature having changed its position.

Pasteur quickly found a way to grow the chicken cholera germs in culture. He placed a few germs in a container of chicken broth and they rapidly multiplied into millions. Next Pasteur and his assistants began routinely feeding the chickens samples of the infected broth in order to study the various stages of the disease. The scientists found that they had to regularly prepare new batches of disease-laced chicken broth. This was because the disease germs in a single container grew weak and died over the course of several weeks.

A Fortunate Mistake

The tendency of the chicken cholera germs to weaken with time was the factor that led to the second bit of chance in Pasteur's discovery. During the summer of 1879 the chemist went on vacation. He ordered his assistants to keep the disease germs alive during his absence by frequently transplanting them to new containers of broth. While their employer was away, however, the assistants decided to take a little vacation of their own, and they neglected the broth cultures. When they returned they injected a chicken with some germs, fully expecting the animal to die. But the chicken remained alive and healthy. Realizing that they had accidentally used weakened germs, the assistants grew a fresh, fully active germ culture and injected it into the same chicken. To their amazement, the bird still did not get sick.

"The Secret Has Been Found!"

When Pasteur returned and learned about the incident, he immediately grasped its significance. The germs from the neglected broth had been too weak to harm the chicken but strong enough to develop the bird's resistance to the disease. Because the chicken had gained immunity, Pasteur realized, the second, more harmful, injection had no effect. "Ah, this is wonderful!" the scientist is said to have exclaimed. "The secret has been found! The old culture protected the hen against the virulent [poisonous] germ. Hens can be vaccinated against chicken cholera." In the following weeks Pasteur and his assistants repeated the experiment many times, always with the same results.

In honor of Edward Jenner, Pasteur called his discovery a vaccine. From then on scientists used the term to describe substances that caused immunity to many other diseases. Though similar

Deep in concentration in his laboratory, Pasteur searches for answers to many important scientific questions of the day.

in principle to Jenner's smallpox vaccine, Pasteur's chicken cholera vaccine was different in one important respect. Jenner's vaccine was derived from a different disease than the one he was trying to prevent. Cowpox was not fatal to humans but triggered the body's immunity to smallpox. Pasteur, on the other hand, had manipulated the very disease germ he sought to prevent. He had shown that chickens developed a resistance to cholera after being injected with a weakened form of the disease itself. This became known as the principle of attenuation.

Pasteur reasoned that if an attenuated vaccine triggered immunity in birds, the same principle should hold true for other animals, including humans. Armed with his new knowledge, he enthusiastically resumed his quest for an anthrax vaccine. Animals with anthrax typically displayed such symptoms as shaking limbs, bleeding from the mouth, and severe convulsions. For several years the disease had killed between one quarter and one-half of the cattle in France annually.

To properly study and experiment with anthrax, Pasteur and his assistants needed to be able to grow cultures of the disease. The method they had used with chicken cholera did not work. Luckily, a German scientist named Robert Koch had recently developed a method for creating cultures of anthrax germs. Koch determined that the tiny organisms multiplied rapidly in fluid taken from the eyes of cattle. Using this method, Pasteur was able to grow large quantities of the disease.

Pasteur heated a solution containing anthrax spores—immature anthrax germs that wait for the right conditions to grow into adult anthrax bacteria. He found that moderate heat weakened the spores and that higher temperatures killed them. Because he wanted to weaken the spores so that they could be used in a vaccine, Pasteur exposed some spore samples several times to moderate

Pasteur developed a vaccine against anthrax even though his microscope could never reveal the clear and precise view of anthrax bacteria that can be seen here.

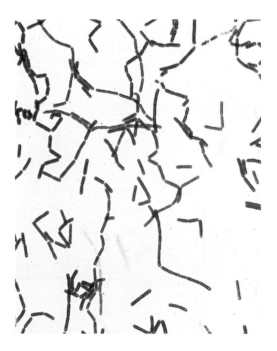

heat. When he tested the weakened germs on lab animals, the results were dramatic. The vaccine successfully made the animals immune to anthrax!

To Pasteur's surprise when he announced his achievement publicly, most veterinarians expressed strong doubts. Some even ridiculed him and his experiment. They were sure that injecting cattle with live anthrax germs would kill the animals rather than make them immune. Also, many of the doctors were jealous and suspicious of Pasteur, whom they looked upon as an outsider to their profession. One French veterinarian, Dr. M. Rossignol, was also the editor of the well-known medical journal *Veterinary Press*. Rossignol wrote sarcastically:

> Will you have some germs? There are some everywhere! The germ theory [and Pasteur's work on vaccines] is the fashion. It reigns undisputed [among the ignorant]. It is a doctrine that must not even be argued, especially when its high priest, the learned Monsieur [Mr.] Pasteur, has pronounced the sacred words, "*I have spoken.*"

Some of Pasteur's supporters suggested that he stage a public demonstration of the new vaccine and, hoping to silence his critics, he agreed.

Putting His Reputation on the Line

The demonstration began on May 5, 1881, in a field at Melun, a village south of Paris. The field belonged to Rossignol, who was only too glad to provide an arena for what he expected to be Pasteur's public humiliation. A large crowd of people, among them other skeptical veterinarians and members of the French press, watched the first stage of the experiment. Pasteur and his assistants divided a group of fifty sheep into two lots of twenty-five each. The sheep in the first lot received the new vaccine, while the other sheep were left untouched. Pasteur's critics were surprised when, in the following week, the vaccinated sheep remained perfectly healthy. They were even more surprised when the animals received a second vaccination on May 17 and still remained healthy. The live germs had not killed the sheep as Pasteur's critics had expected.

Then came the final and crucial stage of the demonstration. On May 31, 1881, Pasteur and his assistants injected all fifty sheep with full-strength, deadly anthrax germs. "A few days later, all vaccinated sheep will be in perfect health," Pasteur confidently predicted. "All unvaccinated ones will be dead." Realizing

German scientist Robert Koch devised a method for growing anthrax germs. Pasteur used the same method to grow large quantities of the disease.

that Pasteur was risking his professional reputation with this bold public experiment, one of his friends remarked:

> You remind me of what a general said about Napoleon—that he liked hazardous games with a touch of grandeur and boldness. It was all or nothing with him. You're carrying on in exactly the same way.

"Yes, I am," Pasteur admitted, and then he returned to Paris, where he spent two sleepless nights waiting for the outcome of the experiment. On the morning of June 2 he received a telegram from Rossignol in Melun urging him to come immediately. "Stupendous success!" the message concluded. Pasteur hurried to Melun, where a huge crowd greeted him. As Madeleine Grant put it:

> Applause and shouts of acclaim rang out as he stepped from the train. Twenty-two of the unvaccinated sheep were dead, and two were barely able to take their last breath. All twenty-five vaccinated [sheep] were in perfect health. . . . The most skeptical joined the applause, and Pasteur was escorted back to the station amid cheers and shouts of "Miracle! Miracle!" Not a person was left to criticize, to doubt.

Afterward Rossignol admitted he had been wrong, apologized to Pasteur, and the two men became friends.

Fighting an Invisible Menace

Having shown that attenuated vaccines worked on animals, Pasteur felt that the next logical step was to try the idea on humans. He began studying hydrophobia, or rabies, a deadly disease usually passed to humans by animal bites. Victims of rabies suffer extreme thirst, choking, convulsions, and almost always death. At the time the only known cure for rabies was to cauterize the wounds— burn them with a red-hot iron—in hopes of killing the infection on the spot. Unfortunately, even this tremendously painful procedure was only occasionally successful.

Pasteur's work with rabies was slow and painstaking. In vain he searched for the menacing disease germs under his microscope. Eventually he concluded that these germs were invisible because they were many times smaller than the bacteria he was used to dealing with. Years later other scientists would confirm this conclusion and name these tiny germs viruses. Despite his inability to see the rabies viruses, Pasteur wisely proceeded under the assumption that they did exist. He was unable to find a way to grow the germs in culture. But he discovered that he could produce a constant supply of the disease for study by cycling it through generations of laboratory rabbits. Cycling is a process through which a researcher infects one animal after another to ensure fresh supplies of the disease.

Pasteur Tests a Rabies Vaccine

After more than four years of experimentation, Pasteur succeeded in attenuating rabies by drying out the spinal cords of rabbits that had died of the illness. Spinal cords dried for only one day, he found, contained germs that were still deadly. Spinal cords dried for fourteen days, however, yielded weak-

Pasteur injected dogs with increasingly stronger doses of rabies to see if they developed resistance to the disease.

Pasteur found that he could maintain a constant supply of rabies germs for study by cycling the germs through generations of laboratory rabbits.

ened, harmless germs. Pasteur injected test dogs with several doses of rabies, beginning with the most attenuated germs and graduating to more deadly ones. During this series of vaccinations the dogs gained increased resistance to rabies until they were immune to it. Pasteur repeated the experiment on 125 dogs. All of them eventually received injections of full-strength rabies, and none of the animals contracted the disease.

A Life-and-Death Situation

By March 1885 Pasteur was nearly ready to try the vaccine on a human being, and he considered testing it on himself.

In a letter to a friend, he wrote:

> I have not yet dared to treat human beings after bites from rabid dogs. But the time is not far off, and I am much inclined to begin by myself—inoculating myself with rabies, and then arresting the consequences [the onset of the disease], for I am beginning to feel very sure of my results.

A few months later, on July 6, Pasteur encountered an unexpected life-and-death situation that eliminated the need for his testing of the vaccine on himself. A nine-year-old boy named Joseph Meister, accompanied by his mother, appeared in Pasteur's laboratory. Two days earlier the boy had been bitten at least fourteen times by a rabid dog. A doctor had cauterized the

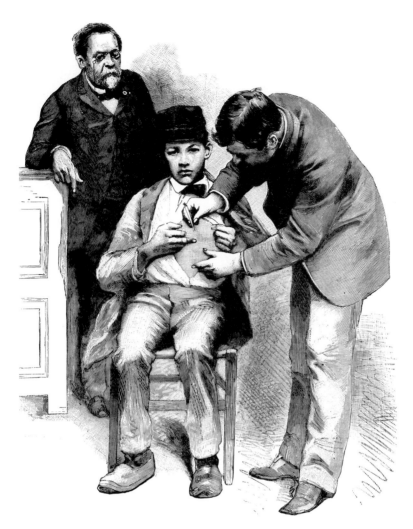

Dr. Jacques Grancher administers a rabies vaccine to Joseph Meister as Pasteur looks on. The nine-year-old boy received twelve injections over the course of ten days and, miraculously, survived without ever contracting the disease.

wounds, but some were very deep and he doubted that young Joseph would live. Having heard about Pasteur's recent success in vaccinating dogs against rabies, the doctor urged Mrs. Meister to rush her son to Paris. If anyone could save the boy, said the doctor, it would be Pasteur.

Pasteur wasted no time. He consulted some medical friends who were familiar with his rabies work, including Dr. Jacques Grancher. They agreed that Pasteur's vaccine was Joseph's only hope, and the treatment began immediately. Because Pasteur was not a medical doctor, he could not legally treat humans, so Grancher gave the boy the initial injection. The boy received twelve shots over the course of ten days, each dose containing stronger and more lethal germs than the last.

After the conclusion of the treatment, there was nothing else to do but wait. If the treatment failed, the boy would come down with the disease within two to ten weeks. Pasteur was nervous but hopeful. "All is going well," he wrote, "the child sleeps well, has a good appetite. . . . If the lad keeps well during the following weeks, I think the experiment will be sure to succeed." Weeks passed, then months. To everyone's relief Joseph Meister remained in excellent health. Pasteur had shown that attenuated vaccines could be used successfully to treat infected human beings.

A Grateful Humanity

Pasteur's work with germs, especially his development of attenuated vaccines, was one of the greatest scientific achievements in history. He not only saved the French fowl and cattle industries, but also rescued those who contracted rabies from terrible suffering and almost certain death. Even more important, Pasteur's observations and discoveries opened the way for new research on vaccines and the eradication of disease. His observations and methods became the tools with which his successors attacked and defeated many disabling or fatal illnesses. Thus, tens of millions of people in subsequent generations who were treated with vaccines indirectly owed their lives to Pasteur and his efforts.

Pasteur lived long enough to receive the gratitude of some of his fellow human beings. On the occasion of his seventieth birthday in 1892, there were celebrations in cities around the world. Tens of thousands of scientists, dignitaries, and ordinary citizens gathered in Paris to honor the man who had saved the lives of so many others. The French government created and distributed special medallions bearing Pasteur's profile and the words: "To Pasteur on his seventieth birthday. France and Humanity [are] grateful." Approaching Pasteur in front of a huge crowd of well-wishers, the great doctor and researcher Joseph Lister summed up the importance of his colleague's work. Said Lister to Pasteur, "You have raised the veil which for centuries had covered infectious diseases."

The Science of Immunology Expands

The work of Pasteur and other scientists of his day opened the way for new research into vaccines. First, Pasteur's work with chicken cholera, anthrax, and rabies vaccines erased all doubts about the worth and potential of the technique of vaccination. Pasteur completely won over those scientists and doctors who previously had been skeptical about vaccination for diseases other than smallpox. The days when re-

Pasteur's work with chicken cholera, anthrax, and rabies erased all doubts about the value and potential of vaccines.

searchers like Jenner and Pasteur had to spend much of their time defending their work were over. All members of the medical and scientific community were now united in the belief that it might indeed be possible to eradicate many deadly diseases. Governments and universities began encouraging and providing funds for new research. The new science of immunology quickly expanded as many medical researchers, young and old, devoted their lives to the study of immunity and vaccines.

New Tools

Pasteur's work with vaccines laid a solid groundwork for these new immunologists. His observations, conclusions, and lab techniques became their basic tools. In the two decades following Pasteur's death in 1895, immunologists used these tools to study many diseases. As research in labs around the world expanded, the scientists made numerous new and important advances. Using Pasteur's procedures, they developed several new vaccines made from live attenuated germs. They also found that the nature and characteristics of different diseases vary a great deal. Therefore, the nature of the vaccines developed for these illnesses must also vary.

Pasteur himself had suggested that attenuated vaccines might not work on every disease. His successors found that he was right and developed alternative types of vaccines, called killed vaccines and toxoids. Immunologists also discovered new ways to grow cultures of disease germs, making it easier to study the germs and develop vaccines.

Assembling the Immunity Puzzle

Perhaps the most important of the initial advances in immunology was the discovery of how the body's immune system works. Jenner and Pasteur had established the basic principles of immunity and vaccines. They had shown that injecting animals and people with mild forms of a disease can build up a tolerance to that disease. But these scientists did not understand how the body builds up such tolerance. In Pasteur's time little was known about the different types of germs and what these tiny organisms did once they entered the body. Scientists also understood little about the cells and processes the body uses to fight germs and create immunity. Therefore, as late as the mid-1880s, when millions of people were benefiting from Pasteur's vaccines, no one knew *how* and *why* these substances actually work.

Inspired by Pasteur, several scientists set out to discover how the immune system works. They reasoned that understanding how the body fights and builds up tolerances to disease would make it much easier to develop preventive measures, including vaccines. The most prominent of these researchers was a Russian biologist named Elie Metchnikoff. Metchnikoff studied the puzzle of immunity on his own during the 1880s. In 1892 he joined the staff of the Pasteur Institute in Paris, a medical

Russian biologist Elie Metchnikoff is one of several scientists whose diligent work led to an understanding of immunity.

research facility established four years earlier. Using Pasteur's accumulated research as a starting point, Metchnikoff carefully studied the body's reactions to various diseases. He also studied body chemistry and cell structure on a microscopic level.

Working separately, other scientists, including German researchers Paul Ehrlich and Emil von Behring, performed some of the same studies and experiments in immunity as Metchnikoff. In a relatively short span of time, these men found and assembled the pieces of the immunity puzzle. By 1908 they had provided a basic picture of

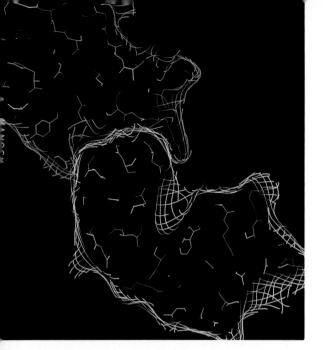

Antibodies are the immune system's weapon against invading antigens. An antibody, outlined in blue, attaches itself to an antigen, outlined in yellow.

stances that invade it from the outside. These harmful substances, most often disease-producing germs, are called antigens. The body's immune response consists of the rapid production of disease-fighting cells and substances to combat and destroy invading antigens.

When an antigen enters the body and triggers the immune response, many different types of cells go to work. First, a type of white blood cell called a lymphocyte, which forms in bone marrow, comes into contact with and recognizes the existence of the antigen. One kind of lymphocyte, the B cell, quickly manufactures special proteins known as antibodies and releases these into the bloodstream. Another kind of lymphocyte, the T cell, does not produce antibodies but helps stimulate the B cell to do so.

The antibodies neutralize the alien

how the body fights disease and how vaccines create immunity. For their landmark explanation of the process of immunity, Metchnikoff and Ehrlich shared the 1908 Nobel Prize for medicine. Other scientists later clarified and added detail to this explanation, especially after the invention of the electron microscope in the 1930s. This device allowed scientists to study tiny germs and body cells that had previously been invisible even through the most powerful microscopes. Thus, research by many scientists over the course of several decades has given immunologists a clear idea of how vaccines provide immunity to disease.

Repelling Foreign Invaders

Vaccines prevent disease by stimulating the body's immune response. This is the body's reaction to harmful sub-

Emil von Behring of Germany independently did many of the same studies done by Metchnikoff and came up with similar conclusions.

THE IMMUNE SYSTEM

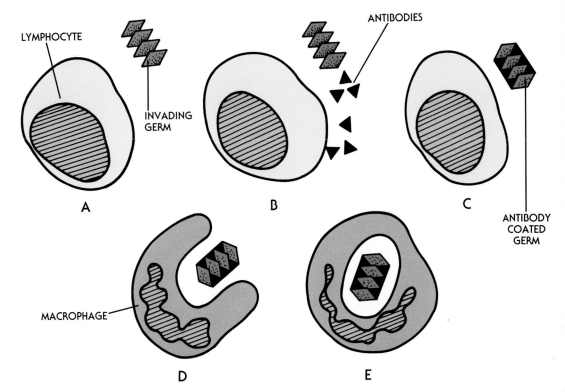

The human immune system is the body's mechanism for fighting disease. When hostile, foreign germs enter the body, the immune system responds. It mounts an attack on the invading germs in an effort to keep the body healthy.

Vaccines trigger this same response through inoculation. Inoculation introduces disease germs into the body, usually in killed or weakened form. Because they have been killed or weakened, the germs pose no real danger. The immune system does not know this, however, and responds by mounting its usual attack. In the process, the immune system learns to recognize this type of germ so that anytime it enters the body the immune system will fight it off. In this way, vaccines create immunity and thus prevent disease.

To repel the invasion of a foreign germ, the body must first recognize the germ as foreign (A). This function is performed by a type of white blood cell known as a lymphocyte. Once it has identified an invading germ, the lymphocyte releases disease-fighting proteins, known as antibodies (B). The antibodies swarm over the invading germ, clinging to it, and forming a coating that prevents the germ from harming the body (C).

After the antibodies have attacked the germ, another type of white blood cell, known as a macrophage, joins the battle (D). The macrophage wraps itself around the antibody-coated germ and then breaks it down into harmless chemicals (E).

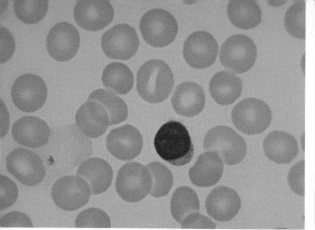
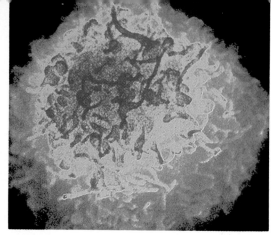

When an antigen enters the body and triggers the immune system, the lymphocytes go right to work. A lymphocyte is visible (left) in a microscopic view of human blood. (Right) A computer-enhanced view of a T-cell type of lymphocyte infected with the AIDS virus.

antigen in one of several ways. Some antibodies trigger chemical changes in the antigen that cause it to dissolve. Other antibodies attach themselves to and cover the antigen, rendering it incapable of doing any damage to the body. Still other antibodies cause chemical reactions that alter the surface of the antigen. This makes the invader stick to others of its kind, forming large antigen clumps. These clumps usually become prey to another kind of disease-fighting cell called a macrophage.

Macrophages are very large cells produced in the bone marrow, spleen, and liver. Instead of making antibodies, macrophages attack, eat, and digest an invading antigen. After observing macrophages at work Metchnikoff explained: "Those cells are the body's defenders. They devour intruders, not for food but for protection. They are the home defense against invasion." When an immune response begins in one part of the body, Metchnikoff discovered, macrophages quickly travel to the scene and begin devouring antigens. They also help the antibodies by consuming the antibody-induced antigen clumps. This is only one example of how all of the body's different kinds of disease-fighting cells work together to repel a foreign invader.

Natural and Artificial Immunity

In addition to fighting an invading disease, the cells marshalled in the immune response also work to protect the body against further attacks of that disease. This is how the body builds what immunologists call active immunity. Acquiring active immunity to disease is possible because the B cells that make antibodies have the ability to "program" themselves to a specific antigen. In other words, once an antigen of a certain disease stimulates the production of antibodies to fight it, the B cells can later recognize another antigen of that same disease. When a person suffers a second infection of the disease, the cells of the immune system react much more quickly than they did the first time. Programmed cells also trigger an immune response to a much smaller number of antigens of the same disease. Because the second immune response is faster

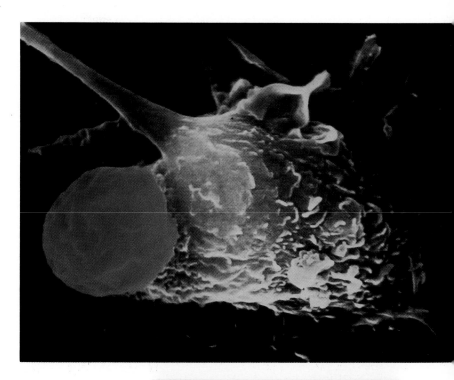

A macrophage, highlighted in brilliant yellow, devours an invading cancer cell.

and stronger, it eliminates the infection before it can spread and the person does not contract a serious case of the disease. The person's body is now immune to infection by that disease.

However, the amount of time the body retains its active immunity varies from disease to disease. Immunity to some diseases lasts for life. For example, if a person survives an attack of yellow fever, his or her immune system will provide permanent protection to yellow fever antigens. Attacks of measles and mumps also impart lifelong immunity. On the other hand some diseases, like the common cold, are caused by hundreds of similar, but different, antigens. Fighting off an infection of one of these will not provide immunity to the others, so a person can catch a cold again not long after the first attack. Another illness that imparts only temporary immunity to those who contract and survive it is influenza, more commonly known as flu.

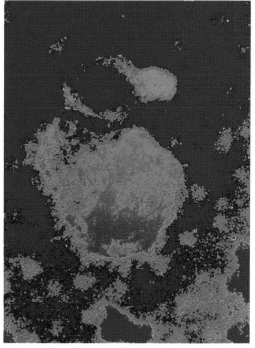

Exposure to some diseases leaves the body with a lifelong immunity. The measles virus, shown in the color-enhanced view above, is one such disease.

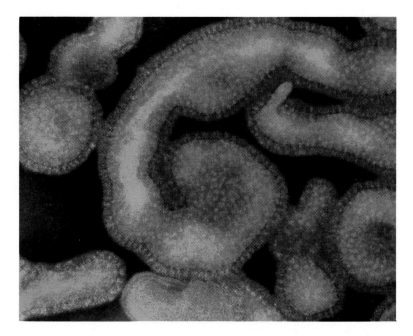

The influenza virus (pictured) triggers only temporary immunity in those who contract it. This means that a person can get the flu over and over again.

When a person catches a disease, recovers, and develops active immunity, that immunity is said to be naturally acquired. For example, the people through the ages who survived attacks of smallpox usually did not catch it again because they had acquired natural immunity to the disease. Similarly, the milkmaids observed by Jenner were immune to smallpox after they had contracted cowpox. The cowpox antigens triggered an immune response that programmed the B cells to recognize those antigens. It happens that the antigens of cowpox and smallpox trigger nearly identical immune responses. Therefore, exposure to cowpox gave the milkmaids a naturally acquired active immunity to smallpox.

As Jenner correctly reasoned, a person can also develop active immunity artificially, that is, by inoculation. When he injected people with cowpox, it triggered the same immune response that would have occurred if they had acquired the germs naturally. Pasteur used the same idea, but carried it a step further by purposely attenuating the germs in his vaccines. These weakened antigens were easily destroyed by the body's onslaught of lymphocytes, antibodies, and macrophages. The vaccinated person experienced only mild symptoms of the disease or no symptoms at all. Though weakened, however, the invading antigens still triggered an immune response in which the body's defenses were programmed for future attacks. Thus, the vaccines imparted active immunity. This is why immunologists often refer to vaccination as active immunization.

The explanation of how immunity and vaccines actually work was a milestone in medical science. Later researchers who studied diseases and searched for ways to prevent them owed a debt of gratitude to Metchnikoff, Ehrlich, and their colleagues. But perhaps no one was more appreciative than Louis Pasteur, who lived just long enough to learn of some of these revo-

HOW VACCINES ARE PREPARED

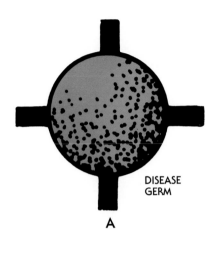

DISEASE GERM

A

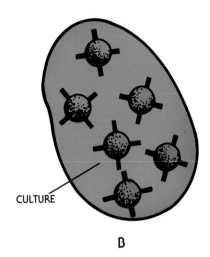

CULTURE

B

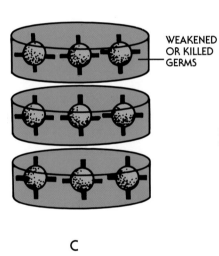

WEAKENED OR KILLED GERMS

C

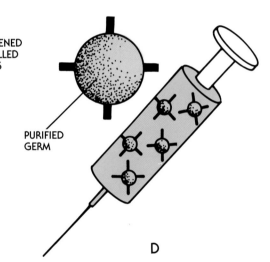

PURIFIED GERM

D

Vaccines can be prepared in different ways. The most basic forms of vaccines use germs that have been weakened or killed. Weakened and killed germs are able to stimulate the immune system, but they pose no serious risk of infection and are easily destroyed by the immune system's disease-fighting cells.

Whichever form of vaccine is used, the steps of production are similar. First, disease germs must be isolated from the tissue or blood of an infected person or animal (A). The isolated germs are placed in material, known as a culture, that serves as food for the germs. The germs eat, grow, and reproduce in the culture (B).

The germs are then weakened or killed. This can be accomplished in various ways including exposure to heat, chemicals, or radiation (C). Once the germs are weakened or killed, they are purified for use in a vaccine (D).

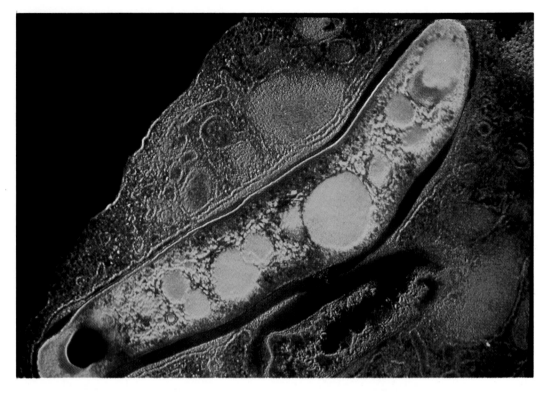

A macrophage envelops a tuberculosis bacterium. Scientists learned that killed disease germs still retain chemical properties that can be detected by macrophages and other cells.

lutionary discoveries. The overjoyed Pasteur told Metchnikoff, "You have explained to me *why*, when a person has had a mild attack of a disease, he cannot get it again. You have explained why my vaccine works as it does, to give immunity."

Killed Vaccines

At the same time that Metchnikoff and his colleagues were solving the riddle of immunity, other scientists were developing new kinds of vaccines. The live attenuated vaccines developed by Pasteur had proven to be effective. And in most cases they appeared to impart long-lasting immunity. But these vaccines had

one drawback. Because the germs in the vaccines were alive, there was a small but ever-present chance that a vaccinated person might actually come down with the disease and die. Immunologists now know that this is because a small percentage of people have impaired or weakened immune systems. Because they have trouble fighting off any kind of infection, even the weakened germs in an attenuated vaccine might be deadly. Other people at risk include pregnant women, whose unborn children might be infected, as well as those allergic to various substances in vaccines.

Pasteur was aware of this problem. After developing his live rabies vaccine he performed further experiments with rabies. He showed that the germs could be killed, and thereby rendered completely harmless, by treating them with chemicals. Yet, for reasons Pasteur did not understand at the time, the "killed" vaccine still stimulated the development of immunity. This observation by Pasteur inspired other scientists. They explored the possibilities of killed vaccines as a safer alternative to live versions for patients with higher risk of infection.

From Animals to Humans

In the mid-1880s two teams of researchers working separately tried to develop a killed vaccine for hog cholera, or swine fever. This disease, which often killed pigs on farms in many areas of the world, was also lethal to many other animals. Working in the United States, Elmer Salmon and Theobald Smith killed hog cholera germs with chemicals and injected them into pigeons. The pigeons quickly developed immu-

nity to the disease. Two of Pasteur's former assistants, Pierre Roux and Charles Chamberland, performed the same experiment in France, also successfully.

In the following years scientists extended the same principle to human diseases. They developed killed vaccines for cholera, bubonic plague, and tuberculosis, as well as for other serious diseases that had ravaged humanity for centuries. They also developed other ways to kill the germs, including heat and radiation.

The researchers eventually discovered why killed vaccines work. They found that, although dead, the germs still retain certain chemical properties. The lymphocytes and macrophages in the body have the ability to detect these properties, so the killed germs stimulate an immune response and produce immunity. But the immunity produced by killed vaccines is much weaker than that created by live ones. Therefore, although killed vaccines are generally safer, they are not long lasting. It is usually necessary to receive several follow-up, or booster, shots of killed vaccines to

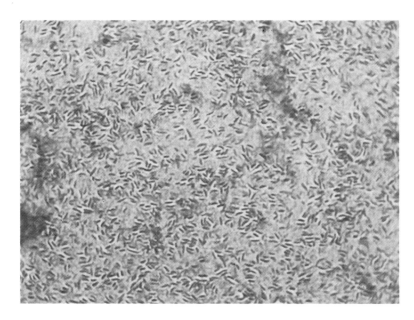

Cholera (pictured) can be prevented with killed vaccines. Because killed vaccines are weaker than live ones, they require boosters to maintain immunity.

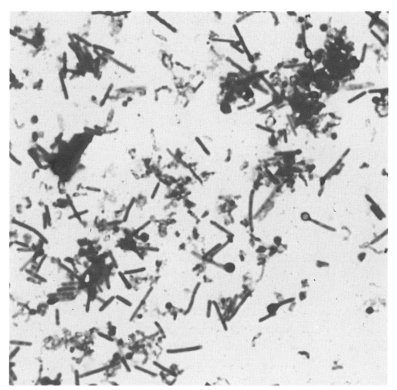

(Right) Tetanus bacteria. Like diphtheria, tetanus requires an antitoxin vaccine. (Below) A child receives a booster shot.

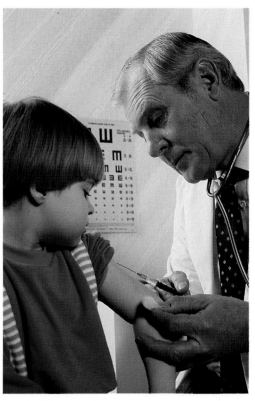

keep the immunity active. Today, both live and killed versions of vaccines exist for many diseases, among them tuberculosis, measles, and rabies. Doctors choose the version they think is most appropriate, considering the patient's risk of infection and other factors.

Defense Against Disease Toxins

While killed vaccines were under development in the late 1800s, scientists studying diseases discovered that germs are not the only kind of harmful antigen. In some illnesses, they found, it is not the disease germs themselves that damage the body. Instead, these germs secrete, or give off, powerful poisons called toxins, which then attack and kill body cells. Among the diseases that

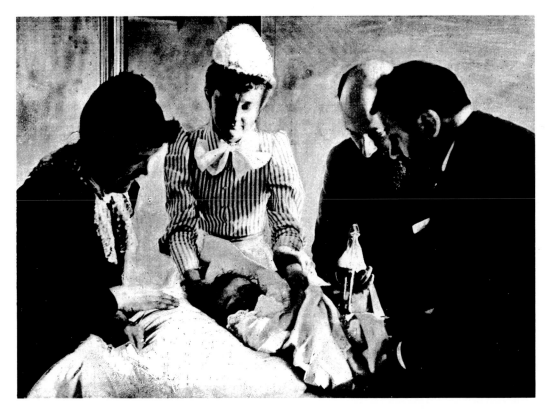

A child is immunized against diphtheria in 1895. This antitoxin vaccine gained widespread use almost immediately because it succeeded where attenuated and killed vaccines had failed.

cause such toxic reactions are diphtheria, tetanus, and botulism. Because the antigens of these diseases are poisons rather than germs, early researchers found that ordinary vaccines made up of germs did not work against them.

A number of scientists responded to the challenge of developing an antitoxin vaccine, or toxoid. Among them were Emil von Behring and Japanese researcher Shibasaburo Kitasato. Working in Germany in the late 1880s, they attempted to find a vaccine for diphtheria. This disease of the respiratory system causes high fever, severe congestion, nerve damage, internal bleeding, and very often death. Large diphtheria epidemics swept Europe and the United States during the nineteenth century, killing millions of people, mostly children.

Behring and Kitasato's first step was to inject guinea pigs with very small amounts of live diphtheria germs. This stimulated immunity in the animals without causing them to contract the disease. The guinea pigs now had in their blood specific antibodies, which Behring and Kitasato called antitoxins, programmed to fight diphtheria toxins. Next, the researchers removed fluid containing antitoxins from the blood of the immunized guinea pigs and injected it into animals that had not been immunized. When the men later injected the second group of animals with

VIRUSES, BACTERIA, AND PROTOZOA

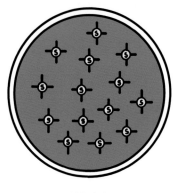

VIRUSES

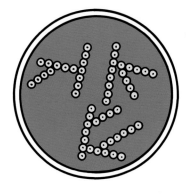

BACTERIA

PROTOZOA

The ease of making a vaccine depends, in part, on the size of the germ being cultured for the vaccine. Large germs, such as the single-celled animals known as protozoa, are easy to see through a conventional microscope and easy to work with in a culture. Bacteria are another type of single-celled organisms that are visible under a microscope and easy to work with because of their size.

Viruses are hundreds and sometimes thousands of times smaller than protozoa or bacteria and much more difficult to work with. A virus is a complex protein molecule capable of invading a living cell and reproducing there. Because viruses are so tiny and because they live inside the cells they invade, they are very difficult to see with a conventional microscope. More powerful microscopes, invented in the twentieth century, finally revealed these tiny organisms to scientists.

Size is not the only obstacle scientists must overcome in creating vaccines to prevent viral diseases. Viruses often change, or mutate, into new forms. This means that vaccine development with one type, or strain, of virus may not work against a newer, mutated form of the virus. This has occurred with various viral illnesses, including influenza. In these cases, vaccines only work for a short time before they are rendered ineffective by changes in the virus.

potent diphtheria toxin, the animals remained unharmed. The antitoxins produced by the first group had stimulated immunity in the second group. After this success, scientists were able to produce antitoxin vaccines in animals and then use these vaccines on humans. The first diphtheria vaccine appeared in 1892, and its use quickly became widespread. Behring received the Nobel Prize for medicine in 1901 for his work on diphtheria.

More advances in toxoids occurred in the twentieth century. Scientists learned to deactivate disease toxins, or render them harmless, by treating them with a chemical called Formalin. When the deactivated toxins are injected into the body, they pose no risk of disease, just as killed vaccines pose no risk of disease. They also stimulate an immune response that produces antibodies programmed to defend against future attacks.

Culturing Deadly Viruses

In addition to creating efficient killed and toxoid vaccines in the late 1800s and early 1900s, scientists continued to develop live attenuated vaccines. The progress made in developing a vaccine for a particular disease often depended on the difficulties of studying and growing that disease. Studying diseases caused by bacteria was relatively easy, because these germs are large and plainly visible under microscopes. Also, scientists found efficient ways to grow bacteria in cultures, giving them sufficient supplies of diseases for study, ex-

perimentation, and vaccine manufacture.

As Pasteur had discovered, working with viruses was much more difficult, partly because these germs are so tiny. Eventually, more powerful microscopes were invented, which revealed these elusive and often deadly germs. For many years, though, no one could find an efficient way to grow viruses in culture. For samples of viral diseases, researchers had to rely on the method developed by Pasteur—cycling the diseases through the bodies of lab animals. Using this procedure makes it difficult to obtain large, concentrated samples of diseases for study and to make vaccines. As a result, progress in developing vaccines for some viral diseases was slow.

In 1949 three scientists working at Children's Hospital in Boston, Mas-

Viruses could not be carefully seen and studied until the development of powerful microscopes.

sachusetts, succeeded in growing viruses in laboratory cultures. John F. Enders, Frederick C. Robbins, and Thomas H. Weller were searching for a way to culture the viruses of infantile paralysis, also known as poliomyelitis, or polio. This disease, which most often strikes children younger than fourteen, can cause crippling paralysis. Enders and his colleagues managed to keep kidney tissues taken from monkeys alive in glass dishes. They infected the tissues with polio viruses, which spread rapidly from cell to cell in the tissues. Eventually the tissue cells died, releasing the viruses and giving the researchers concentrated samples of the germs. Enders, Robbins, and Weller shared the 1954 Nobel Prize for medicine for their achievement.

The achievement had enormous impact for research into all diseases caused by viruses. Now, it was not only much easier for scientists to study and experiment with these diseases, but also easier for them to manufacture viral vaccines. Research on and production of new viral vaccines greatly accelerated. In particular, the work of Enders and the others opened the way for a massive effort to find a safe and reliable vaccine for polio. Scientists would combine the knowledge and techniques contributed by Pasteur, Metchnikoff, Behring, Enders, and many others in an all-out assault on the number one crippler of children.

The Battle Against Polio

The conquest of polio using vaccines was one of the most dramatic medical achievements of the twentieth century. However, researchers and doctors have not completely eradicated polio, as they have smallpox. Polio still occurs each year in various parts of the world. Yet, through the development of safe and effective vaccines, scientists learned to control this crippling illness. In less than two decades polio went from being one of the most widespread and feared

Polio struck terror in the hearts of many people because its victims were most often children. Pictures of children with polio helped mobilize the research effort.

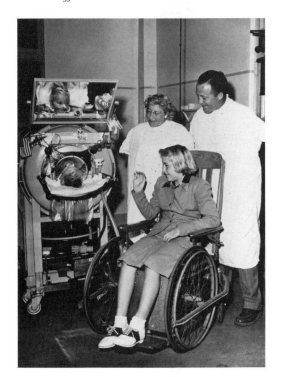

diseases in the world to one of the rarest.

The credit for this achievement goes to many researchers working in laboratories in several countries over the course of decades. To develop successful vaccines against polio they utilized all of the diverse knowledge gained by immunologists in the early 1900s. They also used newer discoveries, such as the laboratory virus cultures grown by John Enders and his colleagues. The defeat of polio was not easy. There were numerous failures and disappointments along the way. But the researchers refused to give up and the result of their dedication is a future in which children no longer need fear the pain and paralysis of polio.

More Frightening than the Atom Bomb

The major reason that so many doctors and researchers sought a prevention for polio was that it was a particularly frightening disease. This was partly because of what it does to those who contract it. In serious cases of the disease the victim first experiences pain in the back and limbs. This soon leads to partial or total paralysis, usually of the lower half of the body. The affected muscles then atrophy, or become weak and useless. Sometimes the disease spreads to the respiratory or nervous systems, causing extreme difficulty in

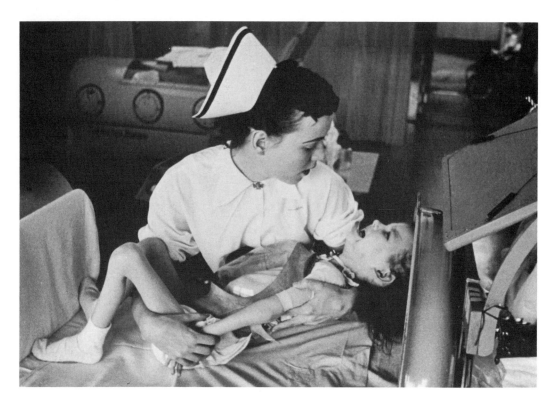

Polio leaves its mark in many ways. It can cause paralysis, extreme difficulty in breathing, and death. A nurse helps a polio-afflicted child, who breathes with the help of a respirator.

breathing, swallowing, and talking. And sometimes death results. Because no cure yet exists for polio, victims who do not die are permanently crippled. Those with milder cases sometimes regain partial use of their limbs through physical therapy involving special exercises. But many victims are confined to beds and wheelchairs for life.

Another reason that polio was so frightening was that it struck so many people, especially children. In 1916 the United States experienced its first large epidemic of the disease. Doctors reported 28,767 cases, 6,000 of which resulted in death. After that, polio attacked the United States every year in what seemed like a never-ending epidemic. There were 25,698 cases in 1946,

42,033 in 1949, and a staggering 57,879 in 1952. "There is literally no acute disease at the present day which causes so much apprehension and alarm in the patient and his relatives," wrote one prominent doctor in 1954. An article in the *Saturday Evening Post* stated, "Polio—a word that strikes more terror in the hearts of parents than the atom bomb." A doctor working at Los Angeles County Hospital wrote to his wife, "People are hysterical, the interns, nurses, and helpers are scared to death and have one or two cases among themselves each day. Fifty admissions every day—everyone strained and worried."

The fact that polio was a frightening and widespread disease was not the only driving force behind the effort to find a polio vaccine. That effort could not have succeeded without a great deal of money to pay for trained researchers, laboratories, and modern medical equipment. A mass movement to raise money for polio research began when Franklin D. Roosevelt was elected president of the United States in 1932. Roosevelt had been struck by polio in 1921. He later recalled:

> When I swung out of bed my left leg lagged. But I managed to move about to shave. I tried to persuade myself that the trouble with my leg was muscular . . . but presently, it refused to work, and then the other [leg failed].

Roosevelt became permanently crippled but, through great courage, went on to become governor of New York and president of the nation. His fight

President Franklin D. Roosevelt was stricken by polio in 1921. His courage inspired many people around the world.

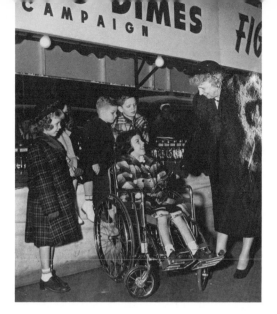

Millions of Americans collected dimes for polio research and contributed them to the March of Dimes. Bess Truman, wife of President Harry Truman, opens the 1950 fundraising campaign.

against the disease inspired many Americans to give money each year to an antipolio fund. Millions of people sent dimes to the White House in the huge fund-raising campaign that became known as the March of Dimes. The tens of millions of dollars collected in the 1930s and 1940s in this effort paid for the eventual development of the successful vaccines that defeated polio.

The Early Failures

The early large-scale research programs that tried to make a safe polio vaccine were unsuccessful. The first occurred in the early 1930s in New York City under the direction of John Albert Kolmer. Kolmer used Pasteur's method of attenuating a live vaccine. The goal was to weaken the polio virus enough so that it would trigger a successful immune reaction without causing the disease. First Kolmer attenuated the virus by cycling it through the spinal cords of living monkeys. Then he further weakened the virus by treating it with a chemical called ricin. Kolmer tested this vaccine on monkeys, and when it appeared to work he vaccinated several human subjects, including himself. When none of his test subjects contracted polio, Kolmer was convinced that he had created an effective vaccine.

In 1935 Kolmer announced his success and launched a vaccination program that began with the inoculation of more than ten thousand children. Almost immediately it was clear that the treatment was a failure. Kolmer was shocked and dismayed when ten of the children came down with polio and five of them died. Dr. James P. Laeke, of the U.S. Public Health Service, investigated the incident and declared that Kolmer's vaccine had caused the children to contract polio. At a meeting of the American Public Health Association that year, Laeke implored Kolmer to withdraw the vaccine from circulation. The saddened Kolmer agreed, saying, "Gentlemen, this is one time I wish the floor would open up and swallow me."

At the same time that Kolmer was conducting his research, two other American scientists, Maurice Brodie and William H. Park, were also working

Poster children became a common sight in efforts to raise money for research.

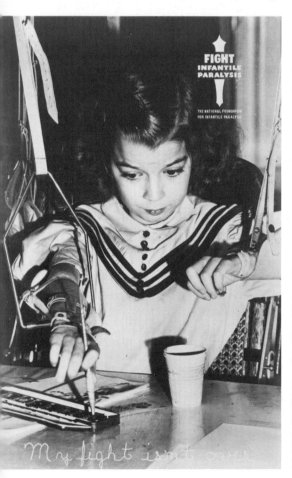

on a polio vaccine. They, too, were convinced that their vaccine, a live attenuated one like Kolmer's, was effective. About 11,200 people, mostly children and nurses, received the Brodie-Park vaccine in 1935. Two of them contracted polio and one died. At the urging of the Public Health Service, Brodie and Park also withdrew their vaccine.

Gathering the Right Tools

Other scientists studied the unsuccessful vaccines in an attempt to discover why they had failed. These studies indicated that the chemicals used to weaken the polio viruses had not affected all of the germs. Some dangerous viruses remained in the vaccines and, when injected into people, caused the disease. Later researchers found another reason the vaccines had failed. Little was known about viruses at the time, and Kolmer, Brodie, and Park assumed that just one kind of virus caused polio. In the 1940s, however, scientists discovered that at least one hundred different polio viruses exist. These fall into three general physical categories, or strains. A vaccine that works with one strain often does not work with another. This partly explains why the Kolmer and Brodie-Park vaccines worked in some instances but not in others.

Because of the failure of these vaccines, many scientists feared that live attenuated polio vaccines were potentially dangerous. Some researchers began to consider the idea of making killed polio vaccines instead. But, whether live or killed, the polio viruses were still difficult to study and impossible to grow in the laboratory. So polio vaccine re-

The National Foundation for Infantile Paralysis chose Dr. Jonas Salk to lead the polio vaccine research effort.

search proceeded slowly during the 1940s.

In 1948 the National Foundation for Infantile Paralysis, established in the 1930s to sponsor polio research, declared an all-out war on the disease. Basil O'Connor, director of the foundation, approached a thirty-four-year-old medical researcher named Jonas Salk. At the time, Salk headed the Virus Research Laboratory in Pittsburgh, Pennsylvania. O'Connor asked Salk to take on the difficult task of studying and classifying all of the different kinds and strains of polio viruses. The study took three years and required some thirty thousand monkeys for growing and testing the viruses. Salk informed O'Connor that any vaccine created would have to work against all three major strains of the disease. At last scientists had a bet-

Salk's first task was to study and classify the different polio virus strains. After completing this three-year effort he set out to find a polio vaccine.

ter understanding of what they were dealing with. Meanwhile, Enders and his colleagues had made their 1949 breakthrough with growing viral cultures in the laboratory. With a clearer idea of the different polio strains and the ability to grow large supplies of them, the scientists now had the tools they needed to make a successful vaccine.

Finding the Right Recipe

O'Connor and others felt that Salk, after completing his detailed study of polio viruses, had a promising chance of making a vaccine. So Salk received generous grants of research money to hire assistants and buy the necessary equipment. In 1951, aided by fifty specialists in immunology, biology, and chemistry, Salk began his quest for the vaccine. He and his colleagues decided to make a killed vaccine because they thought it would be safer to use. For two years Salk worked eighteen hours a day, often

seven days a week. He described his experiments as being similar to someone inventing a new type of cake. The baker "starts with an idea and certain ingredients," said Salk, "and then experiments, a little more of this, a little less of that, and keeps changing things" until the cake is just right.

The first steps of Salk's recipe were to grow all three major strains of polio viruses and then to kill them. Using the Enders method, Salk grew cultures of the viruses in test tubes. He experimented with various chemicals to see which would kill the viruses but, at the same time, leave the germs with the ability to stimulate an immune response in a vaccinated subject. Salk and his associates finally found that a chemical called formaldehyde worked best. When they injected the killed vaccine into test monkeys, the animals produced protective antibodies against all strains of polio. By the middle of 1953 Salk had a vaccine that was effective on monkeys. The next step was to see if it would work on people.

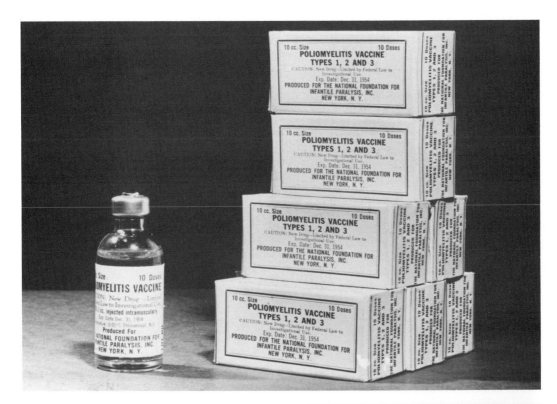

(Above) The vaccine used in Salk's 1954 tests on nearly two million children. In preparation for testing, Salk grew cultures of polio viruses (right) and then searched for a way to kill them without hurting their immune system triggers.

A History-Making Day

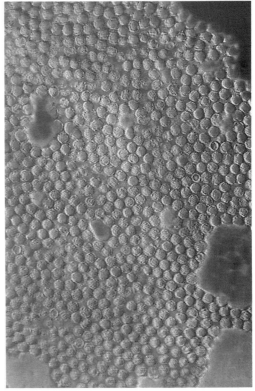

One of Salk's initial tests on humans was to vaccinate himself and his own family. When that and other tests proved successful, Salk told O'Connor that the vaccine was ready for a larger test. While the researchers grew sufficient quantities of the vaccine, O'Connor recruited and organized the subjects for the test. Beginning on April 26, 1954, Salk directed a mass vaccination of 1,829,916 children aged six to nine. Helping in the experiment were 20,000 doctors, 40,000 nurses, 50,000 teachers, and 200,000 adult volunteers. Newspaper reporters called it the greatest mass

Salk vaccinates a child against polio during his 1954 field trials.

test of a scientific discovery in history.

The next steps in the experiment were to monitor the vaccinated children carefully and to examine their reactions to the vaccine. Salk was tense and nervous. "When you inoculate children," he told a friend, "you don't sleep well for two or three months." One thing that consoled Salk was knowing that one of his former college professors, Dr. Thomas Francis of the University of Michigan, would be evaluating the test results. It was Francis who would ultimately determine whether the vaccine was safe and effective enough for widespread use.

After nearly a year of study and evaluation, Francis and his associates were ready with their report. It was April 12,

1955. By coincidence, this was the tenth anniversary of the death of Franklin D. Roosevelt, the man who had inspired the great fight against polio. Salk's biographers, Harold and Doris Faber, described the historic occasion in *American Heroes of the 20th Century*:

> The excitement generated by the Salk vaccine was shown by the elaborate setting for the report's release. On the day it was due, one large auditorium at the University of Michigan . . . looked more like a Hollywood movie set than a campus meeting hall. A battery of sixteen cameras, with shouting crews, focused on the stage from a specially built platform at the rear. . . . Had the vaccine worked? Had the dreaded disease of polio been conquered? . . . At 10:20 A.M., Dr. Francis entered the auditorium. As spotlights blinked on and cameras whirred, he stepped behind a lectern. . . . Adjusting his horn-rimmed glasses, Dr. Francis began to read his report. . . . .The anti-polio vaccine developed by Dr. Salk was safe and effective!

Oveta Culp Hobby, U.S. secretary of health, education and welfare, immediately approved Salk's vaccine for large-scale manufacture by drug companies. "It's a great day," Hobby exclaimed. "It's a wonderful day for the whole world. It's a history-making day." In the following few years, while people around the world hailed Salk as a hero, mass polio vaccinations took place in many countries. These programs proved to be as successful as Salk's initial tests. In the early 1950s tens of thousands of people a year in the United States had contracted polio. In 1961, six years after the vaccine was introduced, only about 500 cases of polio were reported in the United States. Canada reported a drop from over 3,900 cases a year in the early 1950s to only 84 cases in 1961, and the results in many other countries were just as spectacular. U.S. surgeon general Dr. Luther Terry called the success of Salk's vaccine "an historic triumph of preventive medicine."

The Good-Tasting Vaccine

Despite the vaccine's effectiveness many scientists and doctors were not completely satisfied with it. They assumed that, like all other killed vaccines, Salk's would not provide long-lasting immunity. Thus, people would require periodic booster shots to keep their immunity active. This would be costly and also risky, because many people might fail to get their boosters and subsequently contract the disease. So other

Dr. Albert Sabin developed a live polio vaccine that offered long-lasting immunity. He treated the live virus with chemicals to make it safe for use.

researchers worked to develop a live attenuated polio vaccine that would offer more long-lasting immunity.

Among them was Dr. Albert B. Sabin, of the University of Cincinnati College of Medicine. Sabin wanted to avoid the mistakes made with live germs by Kolmer, Brodie, and Park. Some of the viruses in their vaccines had not been properly attenuated, so they infected some of the people who received them. Sabin's goal was to make a live vaccine that would not retain any still-potent germs that might infect people. He did this by treating the polio viruses with chemicals that caused mutations, or physical and genetic changes, in the offspring of the germs. The mutated viruses Sabin created were much weaker than the normal viruses and produced no harmful effects in those vaccinated.

The Sabin polio vaccine has three significant advantages over the Salk version. First, because the germs in the Sabin vaccine are living, they stimulate a stronger immune response, which then imparts stronger, longer-lasting immunity. Second, once the living viruses from the vaccine are in a person's body, that person can transmit them to other people. Because these germs are so weak, they are not dangerous, but they can potentially stimulate the other people to develop immunity. This indirectly extends the chain of immunized subjects. The third advantage of Sabin's vaccine is that it is easier and less painful to administer because it can be taken orally. A killed vaccine like Salk's cannot be taken orally because the digestive process would break it down and destroy its immunizing power. Living viruses like those in Sabin's vaccine, however, can survive the trip through the digestive system.

So doctors usually administer the Sabin vaccine in a lump of sugar or something else that tastes good.

Gaining New Confidence

After the Sabin vaccine went through extensive, large-scale tests, doctors in many countries, including the United States, began using it in 1961. Because of its advantages, within a few years it became the polio vaccine of choice. However, doctors continued to use the Salk vaccine in cases where they felt the live version posed a risk.

The combined effect of the two vaccines was dramatic. By 1969, polio had nearly disappeared in the United States, Canada, Europe, and Asia. Polio cases in Central and South America dropped too. Lack of access to vaccines complicated efforts to reduce polio in Africa. With minor variations, however, the number of polio cases in most countries has remained very low since the 1960s.

The Salk and Sabin vaccines did even more than conquer polio. The de-

Sabin's vaccine was easy to administer because it could be taken orally. A child takes Sabin's vaccine on a sugar cube (below left). Sabin administers his vaccine in liquid form (below right).

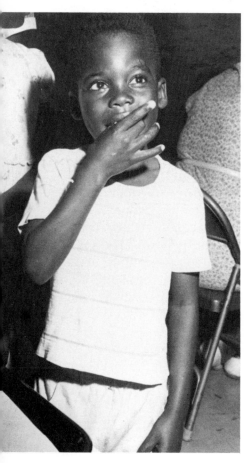

A Columbus, Georgia, police officer is vaccinated against polio. Together, both forms of the vaccine have gone a long way toward someday wiping out polio.

velopment of these vaccines produced many technical advances that helped researchers working on vaccines for other diseases. The successful control of polio also gave scientists and the public alike a new confidence about the ongoing battle against disease. Vaccines seemed to have the potential to someday win the battle. With the goal of fulfilling that potential, vaccine research has expanded in many directions since the 1960s, producing a number of exciting breakthroughs.

CHAPTER 7

A Host of New Vaccines

Most of the many vaccines developed after Pasteur's time were based on the same fundamental principles. They worked by using either weakened or killed versions of disease-causing germs to stimulate protective immunity in the body. In the future scientists and doctors will continue, no doubt, to employ these same techniques when situations warrant.

However, they will also use new types of vaccines, some of which are presently under development in laboratories around the world. The new techniques stem from a deeper understanding of the structure of the human body gained in the latter half of the twentieth century. In particular, modern vaccine research is based on recent discoveries about the makeup of individual body cells and the chemical processes that occur within the cells. Some researchers are focusing on the physical characteristics of disease-causing germs and how these germs trigger antibody production.

Other researchers are delving into the biological mechanisms that direct

Researchers continue their search for new and more effective vaccines. Genetically engineered vaccines are likely to emerge from work done in sophisticated laboratories around the world.

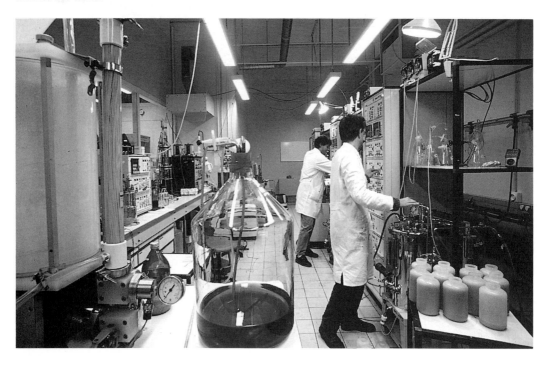

heredity, the process through which characteristics or distinguishing features are passed from parents to children. These scientists have begun to manipulate, or change, these mechanisms, a procedure called genetic engineering. Their goal is to use the products of these experiments to make new and effective vaccines.

Together, these new techniques, along with knowledge of immunology gained over the past century, will enable scientists to do many exciting things with vaccines. They will be able to improve older vaccines. They will be able to develop vaccines that will work against diseases that have been vaccine resistant. Advanced knowledge and technology will allow researchers to create vaccines for diseases that are presently not well understood. In addition, vaccines may someday be used for purposes completely unrelated to disease.

Using Just Part of a Germ

Much of the new vaccine research centers around vaccines that do not use the traditional approach of injecting whole live or killed germs into the body. The first kind of vaccine that departed from this approach is called a polysaccharide. Polysaccharides use just the capsules, or outer shells, that coat some germs, instead of the entire germs. These capsules are composed of carbohydrates, or complex sugars, hence the name polysaccharide—a combination of the words *poly*, meaning "many," and *saccharide*, meaning "sugar." The idea behind these vaccines is that chemicals in the capsules stimulate the body's immune response and trigger the formation of

protective antibodies. But only the entire germs can cause the disease. Therefore, if just the capsules are injected into the body, they can impart immunity without any risk of infection.

Basic research into polysaccharides began in the early 1900s. More intensive research did not occur until the 1960s and 1970s when medical and laboratory technology became more advanced. The first effective polysaccharide developed was a vaccine for bacterial pneumonia, a severe infection of the respiratory system. This vaccine is effective against twenty-three strains of pneumonia, which cause about 90 percent of the cases of the disease in the United States. However, the vaccine is not used very often. This is because most people who

Traditional vaccines were ineffective against bacterial pneumonia because the bacteria (below) form a capsule that protects against the immune system.

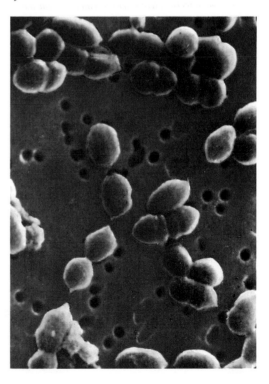

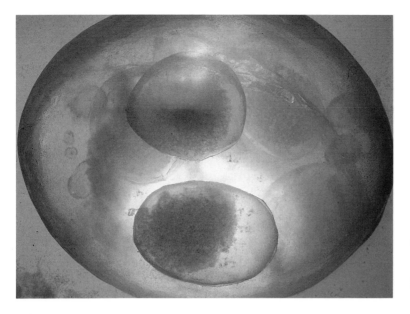

Synthetic peptides offer promise for vaccines against diseases caused by protozoa. One such protozoan appears in this microscopic view.

contract this kind of pneumonia can be treated effectively with a drug called penicillin. So there is no need for large-scale preventive vaccinations. The pneumonia vaccine is most commonly used on people who have a particularly high risk of catching the disease. Researchers continue to study polysaccharides in laboratories around the world. Among the vaccines of this type presently being developed are those for various kinds of influenza and for severe ear infections in children.

Fooling the Body

Scientists are working on other kinds of vaccines that also use individual parts of germs. One of these is called a synthetic, or artificial, peptide. The strategy behind its use is to fool the body into thinking that a disease germ is invading and thus stimulate the production of antibodies. The first step in making the vaccine is to isolate the portion of the germ's surface that triggers the

body's immune response. In a number of germs, this tiny piece of the organism is known as a peptide. Next, researchers synthesize, or manufacture, an exact copy of the peptide using various laboratory chemicals. In theory, when they inject the synthetic peptides into the body, the cells of the immune system will assume that the chemical replicas are the real thing. The cells will then mount a defense and build up immunity. Because they are synthetic they pose no risk of disease.

Many scientists believe that synthetic peptides show much promise for producing vaccines for diseases caused by protozoa. These are very large, complex germs that live as parasites inside the body. Among the many protozoan diseases are malaria, sleeping sickness, and amoebic dysentery. Of these, malaria has recently been targeted by a number of researchers for the development of synthetic peptides. More than 270 million people a year contract malaria worldwide, and about a million of them die every year. This serious disease causes fever, headaches, vomiting, and extreme weakness for several weeks. It can also recur without warning months or even years after the initial infection. This is because the malaria protozoan undergoes several physical changes in the body over the course of time, each of which can trigger a new infection. Stephen Hoffman, director of malaria research at the Naval Medical Research Institute in Bethesda, Maryland, explains:

> Unlike measles or chicken pox, infection with malaria does not give protection against future infections because of the complex life cycle of the malaria parasite. What we have to do using modern molecular biology is something much better than mother nature can do.

Working with a grant from the U.S. Agency for International Development, scientists at the Scripps Research Institute in San Diego, California, are trying to find a vaccine for malaria. One of the most difficult problems to overcome, says Scripps biochemist Arnold Satterthwait, is to form the artificial peptide into the shape that occurs in nature. If the shape is wrong, the immune system cells may not recognize the peptide, and the vaccine might not work. So far the Scripps project has had some limited success in producing antibody protection in test monkeys. However, the researchers are still a long way from producing a successful vaccine for humans. "It's a complex process," says Satterthwait, "and subject to many errors. The final story is not in yet."

Manipulating Life's Hidden Code

Another vaccine that uses just a tiny section of a germ is called a subunit vaccine. Its creation involves techniques of the recently developed technology of genetic engineering. Genetic engineers manipulate the genes, tiny particles inside cells, that carry individual pieces of hereditary information. Genetic engineering developed as the result of the historic 1953 discovery by James Watson and Francis Crick of the structure of the

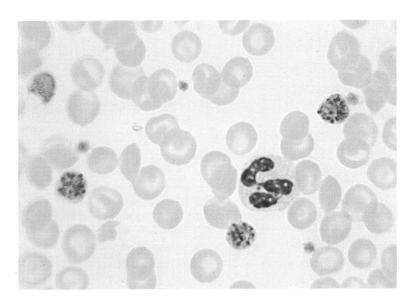

A microscopic view of a malaria parasite. The complex life cycle of the malaria parasite complicates efforts at finding a vaccine.

GENETICALLY ENGINEERED VACCINES

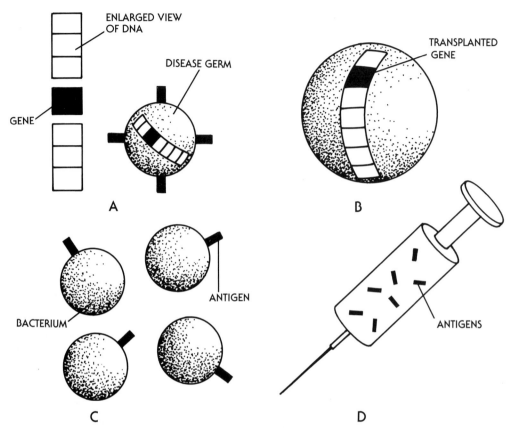

ENLARGED VIEW OF DNA

GENE

DISEASE GERM

A

TRANSPLANTED GENE

B

BACTERIUM

ANTIGEN

C

ANTIGENS

D

Traditional vaccines stimulate the immune system by introducing whole germs into the body. These vaccines work because the immune system reacts to proteins on the surface of the germ, known as antigens. Scientists have also found that they can stimulate the immune system using only the antigens rather than the entire germ. This form of vaccine is thought to be one of the safest because the whole germ never comes in contact with the body.

Antigen vaccines are made through genetic engineering. This is a process of manipulating genes. Genes are complex protein molecules that direct many functions within an organism, including antigen production. Genes are linked together in strands of DNA. DNA contains the code for the millions of types of proteins that make up all living organisms. To make an antigen vaccine, scientists isolate a disease-causing germ and locate the gene that is responsible for producing the germ's antigens (A). Scientists then remove the gene from the germ's DNA. They insert this gene into the DNA of a harmless germ, usually a bacterium (B).

When the bacterium reproduces, so do the antigens thanks to directions from the transplanted gene (C). Because bacteria reproduce quickly, a large number of antigens form. The antigens are then removed from the bacterium and purified for use in a vaccine (D).

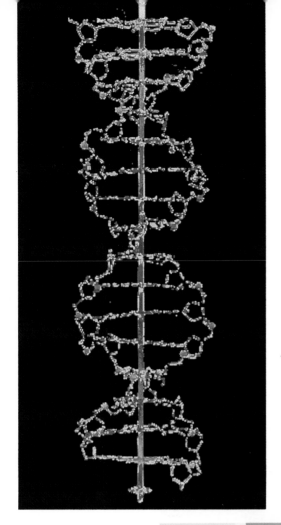

DNA (deoxyribonucleic acid) molecule. This large, highly complex molecule, shaped like a spiral staircase, is the principal component of the genes. The DNA holds the genetic code that specifies all of the characteristics that are passed from parents to children.

The importance of this discovery to the science of immunology has been enormous. By studying the many links in the chain of DNA and its sibling molecule RNA (ribonucleic acid), researchers have been able to isolate a specific gene in some disease germs. This gene, or subunit, contains chemicals that signal the body to form germ-fighting antibodies. These "messenger" chemicals contain DNA from a disease germ and make up subunit vaccines. To make these vaccines the gene containing the chemicals is separated from the germ. Researchers then place the gene in a culture of harmless germs, like baker's yeasts. The DNA of the disease germ and the DNA of the yeasts com-

A computer-enhanced view of the DNA helix (above). Through their studies of DNA, researchers have isolated genes that trigger antibody production. (Right) Scripps Research Institute biochemist Arnold Satterthwait displays models of molecules being used to develop a malaria vaccine.

bine, and the messenger chemicals multiply in the yeasts. When removed from the culture and injected into the body, the chemicals stimulate immunity. But, because the germ itself is not injected, the body does not contract the disease.

The first successful subunit vaccine was the Merck Sharpe & Dohme vaccine for hepatitis B, which the U.S. Food and Drug Administration approved for use in 1986. Hepatitis B is a debilitating disease of the liver and blood often contracted from infected blood during blood transfusions. The vaccine has already proved so effective that doctors in many countries are routinely giving it to infants as a preventive measure. Scientists are presently working on subunit vaccines for Lyme disease, measles, and malaria.

Hope for Preventing AIDS

Subunit vaccines may also hold hope for helping fight acquired immunodeficiency syndrome, or AIDS, caused by the human immunodeficiency virus (HIV). AIDS is a frightening disease that impairs the body's immune system, leaving it open to infection from many other diseases. At present, because no cure or effective vaccine exists, the disease is always fatal. It is spreading rapidly in many countries and some medical authorities fear that over 110 million people worldwide will be infected with HIV by the year 2000.

This unusual disease poses special problems for scientists searching for cures and preventions. Unlike nearly all other diseases, the AIDS virus attacks

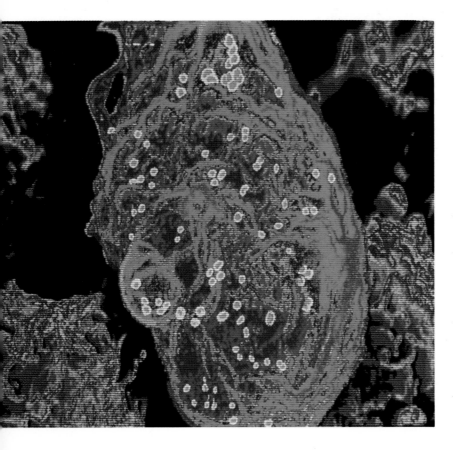

Because the AIDS virus directly attacks the immune system, traditional vaccines are ineffective. At left, the AIDS virus attaches itself to one type of lymphocyte.

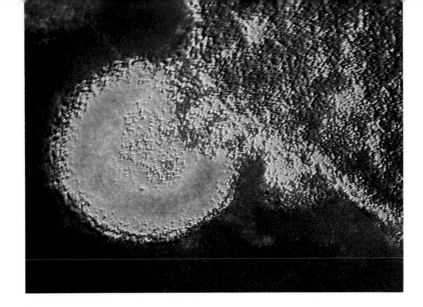

Another computer-enhanced view of the AIDS virus attaching itself to a type of lymphocyte.

the immune system itself, making a normal immune response to the disease impossible. And normal vaccines will not work against AIDS. This is because a vaccine imparts immunity while the body is recovering from a disease. But the body cannot recover when the immune system is not working properly. AIDS researchers Anna Aldovini and Richard A. Young explain:

> The very concept underlying vaccination, reinfection immunity, is not applicable for an infection from which there is no evidence that a person can recover. Researchers do not understand why the immune system can never rid the body of HIV . . . once it has infected a few cells. If the immune system cannot mount an effective response, scientists may not be able to design an AIDS vaccine. The major challenge to developing an AIDS vaccine may well be that HIV infects the very cells, the helper T lymphocytes, that control much of the immune response. . . . And unlike the way infected cells typically respond to most invaders, a fraction of cells carrying HIV may not produce the proteins [messenger chemicals] that alert the immune system.

Because subunit vaccines use genetic engineering to manipulate these messenger chemicals, they offer at least some hope for someday preventing AIDS. Such vaccines are presently under development. A research company called MicroGeneSys in Meriden, Connecticut, is making one that consists of messenger chemicals grown in the laboratory. Once injected, these proteins envelop, or coat the outside of, the AIDS virus. MicroGeneSys researchers hope the proteins will alert uninfected B lymphocytes and stimulate them to produce antibodies to attack the virus. Unfortunately, the researchers say, even if they can make the process work, refining it and testing the vaccine for safety could take years.

Chemicals That Ride in a Vehicle

Because subunit vaccines are made by splitting up and recombining DNA from two different germs, scientists call the technique of creating them recombinant DNA. Another kind of vaccine under development that utilizes this technique is called a recombinant vehicle vaccine. In some ways a vehicle vaccine is like a subunit vaccine. Researchers begin by separating the gene that contains the messenger chemicals from the disease germ and placing it in a harmless germ. In the case of a vehicle vaccine, the second germ is actually injected into the body, becoming the vehicle that carries the messenger chemicals. The cells of the immune system are then stimulated by the messenger chemicals. Because the vehicle germs in the vaccine are harmless, they do not cause an infection.

The main advantage of a vehicle vaccine over a subunit version is that live germs almost always provide the strongest and longest-lasting immunity. Say Aldovini and Young:

> Such vaccines should be more effective than recombinant subunit vaccines because they persist in the body for a longer period, presumably engendering [imparting] a stronger memory for the pathogen [disease germ from which the gene was taken].

The question that most concerns the researchers is, What vehicle will work best? Some scientists are studying cowpox, the disease Jenner used to make his smallpox vaccine, as a possible vehicle. Because the cowpox germ is relatively harmless to humans, it might safely carry the messenger chemicals of a more dangerous disease.

Researchers are also considering a type of bacteria known as BCG as a candidate for a vehicle to carry messenger chemicals. A live attenuated form of BCG has been used for many years as a safe vaccine against tuberculosis. It offers promise for carrying the messenger chemicals of another disease without posing a threat to the body.

Several laboratories are presently engineering BCG germs for possible use in vehicle vaccines. Among the research facilities are Albert Einstein College of Medicine in New York City and the MedImmune Company in Gaithersburg, Maryland. Researchers at these laboratories have injected mice with experimental BCG vehicle vaccines for Lyme disease, tetanus, and malaria. The mice have developed strong immune responses to these diseases. MedImmune has taken the tests a step further by injecting monkeys with a BCG vac-

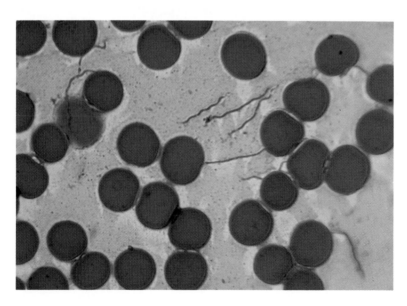

A microscopic view of Lyme disease germs. Researchers are experimenting with a vehicle vaccine for Lyme disease.

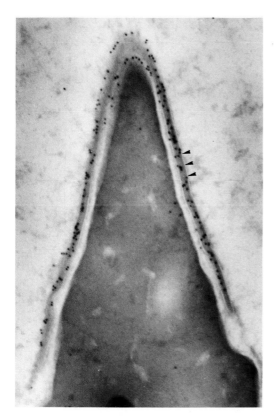

A highly magnified image of a human sperm head reacting with the antibody triggered by the University of Virginia contraceptive vaccine. Gold particles are used to mark the location of the SP-10 protein (shown by arrows).

cine for Lyme disease. Because monkeys are more closely related to humans than are other animals, the results of these tests may give a better indication of how the vaccine will work on people. The researchers hope to develop safe vaccines for human use by the mid-1990s.

Preventing Pregnancy

Genetic engineering has also opened the door to pathways unimagined by any of the early vaccine pioneers. It is unlikely that Jenner, Pasteur, or many of those who followed ever envisioned vaccines serving a purpose unrelated to preventing disease. In fact, this is precisely where some vaccine research is leading.

Scientists in several countries are studying and testing vaccines that someday might be used to prevent pregnancy. Contraceptive vaccines, if successful, could make women immune to pregnancy for several years at a time. One researcher, John Herr of the University of Virginia, predicts that contraceptive vaccines could be a reality by the end of the decade.

The vaccine Herr and his colleagues are working on would trigger a woman's immune system to produce antibodies. The antibodies would bind to proteins found on the surface of the sperm and destroy their ability to fertil-

To prevent fertilization between sperm and egg (below), one vaccine would trigger antibody production in a woman's body. The antibodies would bind to the sperm, preventing fertilization.

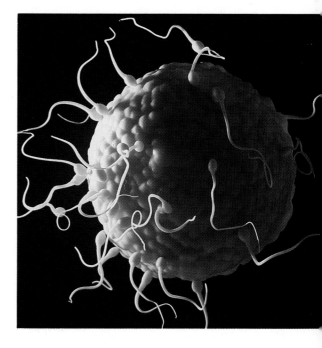

ize the egg. Herr and his colleagues call this sperm protein SP-10.

Early tests on female rabbits have proved successful. Injections of the vaccine stimulated their immune systems to produce antibodies to the sperm protein. Further tests are needed, however, to learn whether the vaccine will actually prevent conception. These tests are being done first on baboons; human testing of the vaccine may still be a few years away.

Human tests have already begun on another antipregnancy vaccine. Scientists in Australia and India are testing a vaccine that prevents implantation of the embryo in the uterus after fertilization has occurred. It does this by triggering an immune response against a hormone produced by the early embryo.

Even if proven safe and effective, this type of vaccine could run into trouble in some countries. Unlike the SP-10 and other similar vaccines that would prevent fertilization, the vaccines undergoing tests in Australia and India act after fertilization. Because of this, some people might consider this vaccine a form of abortion. Because abortion is highly controversial, this type of vaccine might not win universal acceptance.

Beyond Imagination

Nevertheless, the many technical advances and discoveries of the twentieth century—especially the manipulation of the genetic code—have opened the way for the development of a host of new and cleverly engineered vaccines. In the next century scientists will likely create new vaccine technologies that cannot now be imagined. These exciting discoveries may help eliminate many dread diseases that have long plagued humanity. Pasteur's dream of a vaccine for every disease may come true in ways he could scarcely dream of.

Glossary

■■

antibodies: Proteins manufactured by white blood cells to defend against invading disease germs.

antigen: A harmful substance, usually part or all of a disease germ, that invades the body.

antitoxin: A substance that neutralizes a toxin.

artificial immunity: Immunity imparted by purposely injecting the body with a substance, such as a vaccine, that stimulates immunity.

attenuation: The weakening of harmful disease germs for use in a vaccine.

bacteria: Germs that sometimes cause disease.

bleeding: The once-common practice of removing some of the blood from a person's body, based on the false belief that blood contains "impurities."

booster shot: A follow-up vaccination to keep the body's immunity active.

culture: A laboratory growth of germs for medical use.

DNA and RNA: The major components of the genetic materials of living things.

genetic engineering: The manipulation of genetic material, which is responsible for transmitting characteristics from parents to offspring.

genetics: The study of heredity, or the transmission of characteristics from one generation to another.

germs: The general name given to microscopic living things.

germ theory: The concept that germs can cause disease.

immune response: The body's defensive reaction to harmful substances that invade it from the outside.

immunity: The process by which the body resists disease.

immunologist: A scientist who studies the process of immunity and seeks ways to prevent disease.

immunology: The study of the process of immunity and prevention of disease.

inoculation: The practice of injecting the body with a form of a disease to ward off future attacks of the disease.

killed vaccine: A vaccine made of germs that have been rendered harmless by killing them.

live vaccine: A vaccine made of living germs.

lymphocyte: A white blood cell that manufactures or aids in the manufacture of defensive antibodies.

macrophage: A large defensive body cell that destroys harmful antigens.

mutation: An offspring that is significantly different in form from its parents.

natural immunity: Immunity gained by naturally contracting and surviving a disease.

polysaccharide vaccine: A vaccine made of the carbohydrate outer shell of a germ.

pustule: An open sore filled with pus.

recombinant DNA: DNA that has been artificially prepared by combining DNA fragments from different species.

recombinant vehicle vaccine: A vaccine made of harmless germs that have been artificially altered to carry genetic information taken from harmful germs.

strain: A variation of a specific kind of disease germ.

subunit vaccine: A vaccine made of disease antigens that were artificially altered by being grown in cultures of harmless germs.

synthetic peptide vaccine: A vaccine made of artificial chemical copies of parts of microscopic parasites.

tolerance: The body's ability to withstand a disease.

toxin: A poison.

toxoid vaccine: A vaccine made of antitoxins.

vaccination: The process of administering a vaccine.

vaccine: A substance that provides protection against a specific disease by triggering the body's immune system without passing on the disease itself.

virus: A tiny germ that often causes disease.

For Further Reading

■■

Anna Aldovini and Richard A. Young, "The New Vaccines," *Technology Review,* January 1992.

Great Disasters: Dramatic Stories of Nature's Awesome Powers. Pleasantville, NY: Reader's Digest Association, 1989.

Harold Faber and Doris Faber, *American Heroes of the 20th Century.* New York: Random House, 1967.

Madeleine P. Grant, *Louis Pasteur: Fighting Hero of Science.* New York: McGraw-Hill, 1959.

Ruth Fox Hume, *Great Men of Medicine.* New York: Random House, 1961.

Roberto Margotta, *The Story of Medicine.* Edited by Paul Lewis. New York: Golden Press, 1967.

Don Nardo, *Germs: Mysterious Microorganisms.* San Diego: Lucent Books, 1991.

A. J. Harding Rains, *Edward Jenner and Vaccination.* Hove, England: Wayland Publishers, 1974.

Marianne Tully and Mary-Alice Tully, *Dread Diseases.* New York: Franklin Watts, 1978.

Works Consulted

■■

Fred Brown, "Modern Vaccines: From Jenner to Genes—The New Vaccines," *The Lancet*, March 10, 1990.

Allen Chase, *Magic Shots*. New York: William Morrow and Company, 1982.

Logan Clendening, ed., *Source Book of Medical History*. New York: Dover Publications, 1942.

David Graham, "Scripps seeks to develop vaccine to combat resurgence of malaria," *San Diego Union*, May 10, 1992.

Gregory Gregoriadis, Anthony C. Allison, and George Poste, eds., *Vaccines: Recent Trends and Progress*. New York and London: Plenum Press, 1991.

H. J. Parish, *A History of Immunization*. Edinburgh and London: E & S Livingstone, 1965.

Stanley A. Plotkin and Edward A. Mortimer, eds., *Vaccines*. Philadelphia: W. B. Saunders, 1988.

Noel R. Rose, *Principles of Immunology*. New York: Macmillan, 1973.

Joel N. Shurkin, *The Invisible Fire*. New York: G. P. Putnam's Sons, 1979.

Robert Steinbrook, "AIDS vaccine tests fraught with peril," *Los Angeles Times*, June 15, 1992.

C. G. A. Thomas, *Medical Microbiology*. London: Bailliere/Tindall, 1973.

René Valery-Radot, *The Life of Pasteur*. Translated by R. L. Devonshire. Garden City, NY: Garden City Publishing, 1926.

A. Voller and H. Friedman, eds., *New Trends and Developments in Vaccines*. Baltimore, MD: University Park Press, 1978.

Graham S. Wilson, *The Hazards of Immunization*. London: Athlone Press, University of London, 1967.

Graeme C. Woodrow and Myron M. Levine, eds., *New Generation Vaccines*. New York and Basel: Marcel Dekker Inc, 1990.

Index

swine fever (hog cholera), 59
synthetic peptide, 78
TB (tuberculosis), 59-60, 84
T cell, 52, 54
Terry, Luther, 73
tetanus, 60-61, 84
Timonius, Emanuel, 18
T lymphocytes, 83
Toussaint, H., 41-42
toxins, 60
toxoids (antitoxin vaccines), 60-63
Truman, Bess, 67
Truman, Harry, 67
tuberculosis (TB), 59-60, 84
Turkey, smallpox experiments in, 15-16

United Nations, 10
U.S. Agency for International Development, 79
U.S. Food and Drug Administration, 82
U.S. Public Health Service, 68, 69
vaccine(s)
  anthrax vaccine, 43-45
  antipregnancy (contraceptive) vaccines, 85-86
  antitoxin (toxoid) vaccines, 60-63
  chicken cholera vaccine, 43-45
  genetically engineered, 76-77
    how they work, 79-82
  hepatitis B vaccine, 82
  immune system and, 52-54
  killed vaccines, 51, 58-60, 70
  oral (sugar cube) vaccine, 73-74
  polio vaccines, 71-75
  preparation of, 57, 80
  rabies vaccine, 45-49
  recombinant vehicle vaccine, 83-84
  subunit vaccine, 79
  the term, origin of, 26-27, 42
  viral vaccines, 63-65
  why they work, 59-60

Variolae vaccinae, 26
vehicle vaccine, 83-84
Veterinary Press, 44
virus(es), 46
  characteristics of, 62
  culturing of, 63-64
  mutation of, 62, 73
  viral vaccines, 63-65
Virus Research Laboratory, 69

Waterhouse, Benjamin, 35
Watson, James, 79
Weller, Thomas H., 63-64
white blood cells, 52-53
World Health Organization (WHO), 10-11

yellow fever, 55
Young, Richard A., 83-84

About the Authors

▪▪

Michael C. Burge has degrees from Fordham University and the University of Delaware. He has taught as a Peace Corps volunteer in Kenya, East Africa, and has worked as a reporter and editor for newspapers in California and Oregon. He lives in Escondido, California, with his wife and three children, to whom this book is dedicated.

Don Nardo is an actor, film director, and composer, as well as an award-winning writer. As an actor, he has appeared in more than fifty stage productions. He has also worked before or behind the camera in twenty films. Several of his musical compositions, including a young person's version of *The War of the Worlds* and the oratorio *Richard III*, have been performed by regional orchestras. Mr. Nardo's writing credits include short stories, articles, and more than thirty-five books, including *Lasers, Germs, Gravity, Anxiety and Phobias, The Irish Potato Famine, Exercise, Recycling, The Indian Wars, H. G. Wells,* and *Charles Darwin.* Among his other writings are an episode of ABC's "Spenser: For Hire" and numerous screenplays. Mr. Nardo lives with his wife Christine on Cape Cod, Massachusetts.

Picture Credits

■■■

Cover photo by Dagmar Fabricius/Uniphoto

© Becker, PhD/Custom Medical Stock Photo, 54 (right)

© Jan Callagan/Phototake NYC, 63

Carolina Biological Supply, 54 (left), 60 (top), 79, 84

© CNRI/Phototake NYC, 44, 59

CNRI/Science Photo Library, 77

© Electra/CNRI/Phototake NYC, 55 (top)

Barry Fitzsimmons/Union-Tribune, 81 (bottom)

Franklin D. Roosevelt Library, 67 (bottom)

John C. Herr/University of Virginia, 85 (top)

Historical Pictures/Stock Montage, 20, 33 (top), 43, 51

© Institut Pasteur/CNRI/Phototake NYC, 22, 58, 71 (bottom), 83

© Dr. Dennis Kunkel/Phototake NYC, 56

© Lew Lause 1991/Uniphoto, 60 (bottom)

Library of Congress, 12, 15, 17 (both), 18, 19 (both), 21, 25, 27 (both), 28, 34, 35 (both), 36, 38 (top), 39, 40, 41, 45, 50, 52 (bottom)

National Archives, 65, 66, 67 (top), 69, 70, 71 (top), 72, 73, 74 (both), 75

Northwind Picture Archives, 14, 23 (both), 26, 29, 30, 31, 32, 33 (bottom), 37, 38 (bottom), 46, 47, 48, 61, 68 (both)

Philippe Plailly/Science Photo Library, 76

© Claude Revy, Jean/Phototake NYC, 52 (top)

© 1991 Eric Saul/Custom Medical Stock Photo, 81 (top)

© Bob Schuchman/Phototake NYC, 85 (bottom)

© Peter A. Simon/Phototake NYC, 78

© SIU Biomed Comm/Custom Medical Stock Photo, 55 (bottom)

Renata Sobieraj, 53, 57, 62, 80

© Wagner Herbert Stock/Phototake NYC, 82